Border
Clip Art
for
Libraries

Border Clip Art for Libraries

Phil Bradbury

LIBRARIES UNLIMITED, INC.
Englewood, Colorado
1989

LIBRARIES UNLIMITED, INC.
P.O. Box 3988
Englewood, CO 80155-3988

Library of Congress Cataloging-in-Publication Data

Bradbury, Phil, 1946-
   Border clip art for libraries.

   1. Libraries and publishing--Handbooks, manuals, etc.
2. Library publications--Handbooks, manuals, etc.
3. Library exhibits--Handbooks, manuals, etc. 4. Copy
art--Handbooks, manuals, etc. 5. Borders, Ornamental
(Decorative arts)--Handbooks, manuals, etc. I. Title.
Z716.6.B73   1989   025.1'29   89-2306
ISBN 0-87287-744-2

For Kathy, who gave me Meagan,
and for the Muggins herself,
who makes my heart laugh

CONTENTS

ACKNOWLEDGMENTS ix

INTRODUCTION xi

Section I—MEDIA 1

Section II—SIGNS & MEMOS 13

Section III—HOLIDAYS 44

Section IV—ART 73

Section V—UNIQUE BORDERS 96

Section VI—TREASURY 112

INDEX 123

ACKNOWLEDGMENTS

I would like to offer a special thanks to David Keeler, who introduced me to the tools that made this book possible, and to Richard Loggins, for much helpful technical advice.

INTRODUCTION

In *Border Clip Art for Libraries* you will find over 300 complete borders plus headlines and clip art elements to aid in preparing artwork for a wide range of library promotional materials. Not all are different; many have been provided in several proportions and sizes, including reverse designs. They were created to be used with a variety of reproduction techniques and can be employed with equal utility by the library which has access to only a photocopier as well as the library which is lucky enough to be blessed with a fully equipped graphic arts department.

The book is divided into six sections: Media, Signs & Memos, Holidays, Art, Unique Borders, and Treasury. One or more pages of clip art elements from the border designs appear at the front of each section. The Treasury section contains miniature graphics from all sections.

The best way to use this book is to simply familiarize yourself with its contents. A working knowledge of the illustrations and borders will make planning promotional materials a much easier task. Often the designs themselves will suggest projects and generate ideas.

Techniques

The two principal reproduction methods the purchaser of this book is most likely to use are photocopying and photo-offset printing. Photocopying as a printing process has several advantages over photo-offset reproduction. The cost is generally lower, expecially for short runs; editing and making changes is much easier; the time between concept and finished piece is certainly shorter; and there is a greater degree of control over the entire process. The disadvantages of using a photocopier instead of a printing press are lower technical quality; restrictions on the kind, size, and color of paper stock which can be used as well as limitations on the use of colored inks.

If the borders are to be reproduced in a photocopier, be sure to apply a white opaque along the edges of pasted-up elements to avoid shadow lines. Another method of eliminating shadow lines (and a good idea for borders which are used often) is to have the border made into a transparency. Type your copy in position on a page, lay the transparency over the typed copy, and photocopy both at the same time.

The border designs will also work well when reproduced through the use of electronic stencils. To print a border in two colors in an electronic stencil machine, it is not necessary to make two artworks or to prepare an overlay. Simply make two stencils of the entire artwork. With cellophane tape mask out selected areas on each stencil (e.g., mask out the border on one, and the headlines on the other). This will have the added benefit of making proper positioning easier when the second color is run.

All the borders in this book are "line art." They are composed solely of areas of black or white; there are no gray or middle tones such as you might see in a photographic print. If you look closely at what appears to be a gray tint, such as the walking computer on the "Computer Club" border, you will note that what your eye interprets as gray is actually a pattern of small black dots. The smaller and further apart the dots, the lighter the tint appears to be.

For the most part these tinted areas will have no bearing on your selection of a particular design; all will reproduce equally well for a wide range of printed materials. It is a good idea, however, to avoid illustrations with screened areas (as well as drawings with thin lines or much small detail) if you are creating an artwork for a library T-shirt or bookbag to be reproduced by silkscreen.

By combining elements of several different borders or adding and removing items (or both) in an existing illustration, you can create a variety of specialized designs for particular applications. For example, the "Bookmobile" border shown here

can contain the weekly schedule of stops in the six panels provided or the panels (and the door) can be removed so the entire space is available for copy. By adding a square, a triangle, and a round-cornered rectangle to this illustration, it turns from a bookmobile into a motor home and can be used to promote camping and recreation books. Similarly, by moving the door to the rear and adding a set of steps, the illustration can be used to publicize home delivery service (see page xiii).

To make it easy to customize the borders, clip art elements from many of them have been provided on pages preceding each section. Illustrations on these pages have been created in several sizes and in some cases flopped and reversed, or both, to increase their utility.

Camping & Recreation

Be sure to check the Reference Department for more maps and travel guides. Happy Vacation!

NEW BOOKS

HOME DELIVERY SERVICE
Bringing You the Books!

Mondays and Thursdays

Resizing

The borders have been produced in a variety of proportions and sizes, but you will undoubtedly find times when adjustment is necessary. When the proportion of the border is correct for your needs but the size is not, it is recommended that a photostat enlargement or reduction be made. It is a good idea when having a photostat made to fill the area inside the border that you plan to use with pieces of clip art, headlines, other small borders, and so forth. When a border design is enlarged, you are already paying for the "empty space" in the middle of the frame. You might as well put it to good use by having other art elements you might need enlarged along with your selected border.

When the proportions of a border need to be changed, i.e., the width or depth is not the correct size for the task at hand, it is often easiest to leave the corner elements in place and make changes by cutting through the sides of the border. Many of the designs use a straight line or a repeating pattern for their edges, and can easily be adjusted in this manner. Simply position the corners and add or remove portions of the sides to achieve the size you need. When enlarging a design you may need to first make extra copies at original size to provide sufficient pieces of the line or pattern.

Signs & Posters

Enlarging the borders for use on signs and posters can be done in several ways:

Proportional Square Method—The proportional square method is a way for the even non-artistic to create well-drawn, large-scale posters by literally dividing the drawing task into little blocks. It is the most basic and the most laborious means of enlarging an illustration.

A sheet of tracing paper or acetate ruled with squares (½" or 1" on a side) is laid over the item to be enlarged. A second sheet of tracing paper ruled with proportionately larger squares (2" or 3" on a side) is made also. Simply copy the border or illustration square by square. When complete, rub the back of your enlarged drawing with a soft pencil (making it into a sheet of one-time carbon paper). Attach it, face up, to your poster board and go over the drawing with a sharp pencil or stylus to transfer it to your poster.

You can also lightly draw the enlarged squares directly on your posterboard and erase them after your drawing has been inked or painted. The advantage of using the tracing paper is that you then have an original on file and can quickly create additional posters.

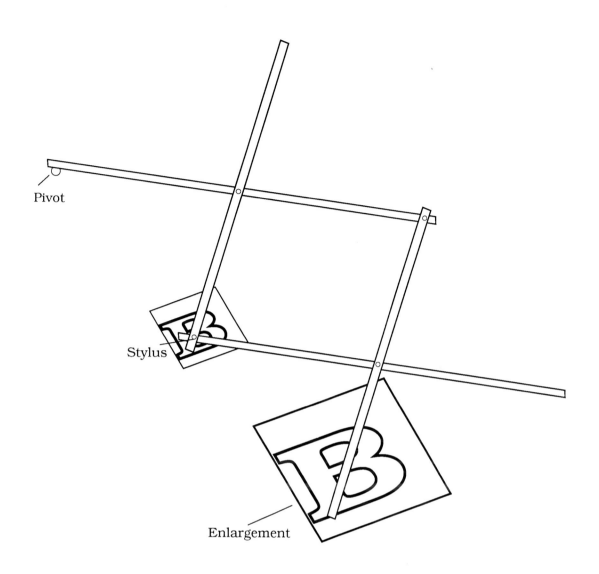

Pivot

Stylus

Enlargement

Pantograph–A pantograph will enable you to enlarge or reduce selected designs in precise size ratios. Once the device is adjusted for the desired size, simply trace the original with the stylus. An enlarged duplicate is produced automatically by a pencil lead set in the reproducing arm of the device.

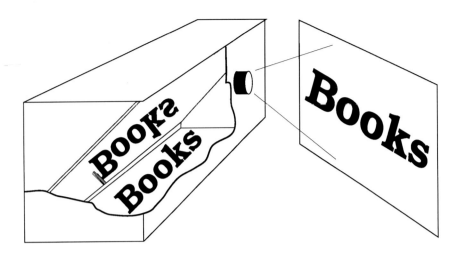

Opaque Projector—One of the fastest and easiest enlarging tools for poster and sign work is the opaque projector. The material to be copied is placed within the opaque projector, and its image is projected onto a poster board attached to a wall or placed on an easel. The image is lightly traced onto the poster with a soft pencil and inked or painted to complete the work. (Designs which have been made into transparencies can be enlarged in a similar manner with an overhead projector.)

Photostats—While easily done, poster-size photostats are expensive and have other drawbacks as well. Your enlargement will be on photostat paper; other items such as lettering and additional illustration must be done on the stat paper. The photostat will then have to be mounted on stiff backing board for display. Dry-mount presses which use heat are not recommended as they will often cause the photostat to bubble and discolor. Stat cameras work in black-and-white. If you wish to have your poster border in a color other than black, another enlarging method may be best.

Finally, while it is not necessary to be an expert in the graphic arts to use this book effectively—indeed, in large part *Border Clip Art for Libraries* is designed expressly for use by people who are not professional graphic artists—a familiarity with the basic tools and techniques of the field will be most helpful in planning and producing printed materials. There are many excellent books available. Three we recommend are *ClipArt & Dynamic Designs for Libraries & Media Centers: Volume 1: Books & Basics* and *Volume 2: Computers and Audiovisual* (Englewood, Colo.: Libraries Unlimited, 1988) by Judy Gay Matthews, Michael Mancarella, and Shirley Lambert and *Complete Guide to Pasteup* (Philadelphia: North American Publishing Co., 1975) by Walter B. Graham.

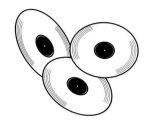
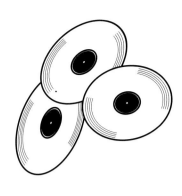

Section I
MEDIA

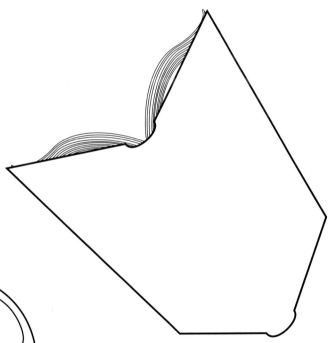

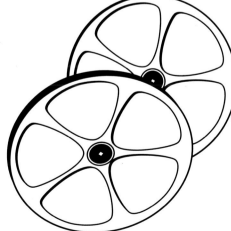

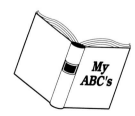

My ABC's

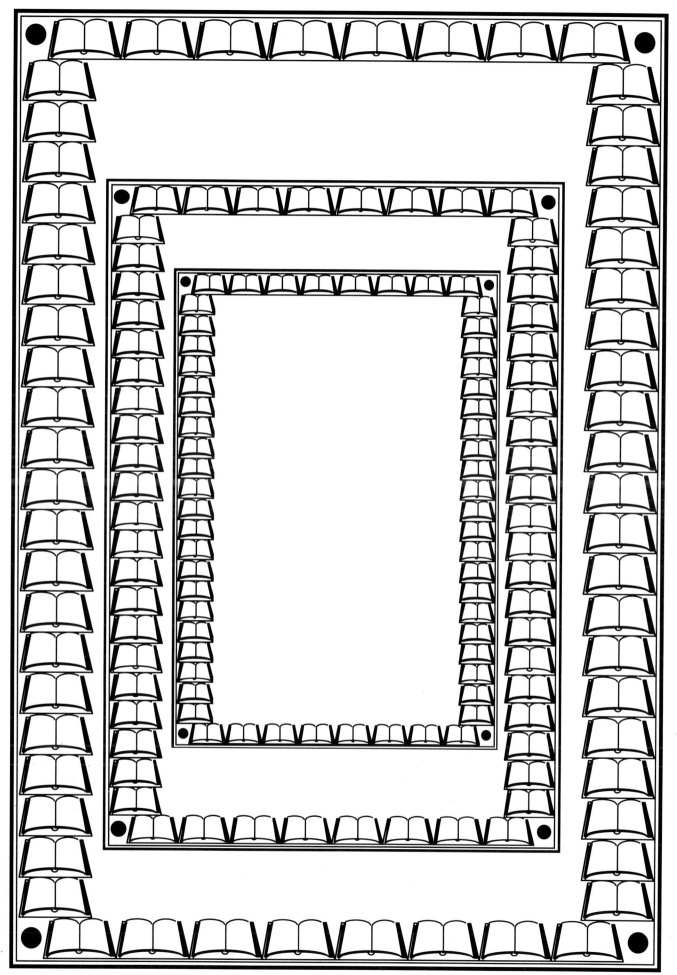

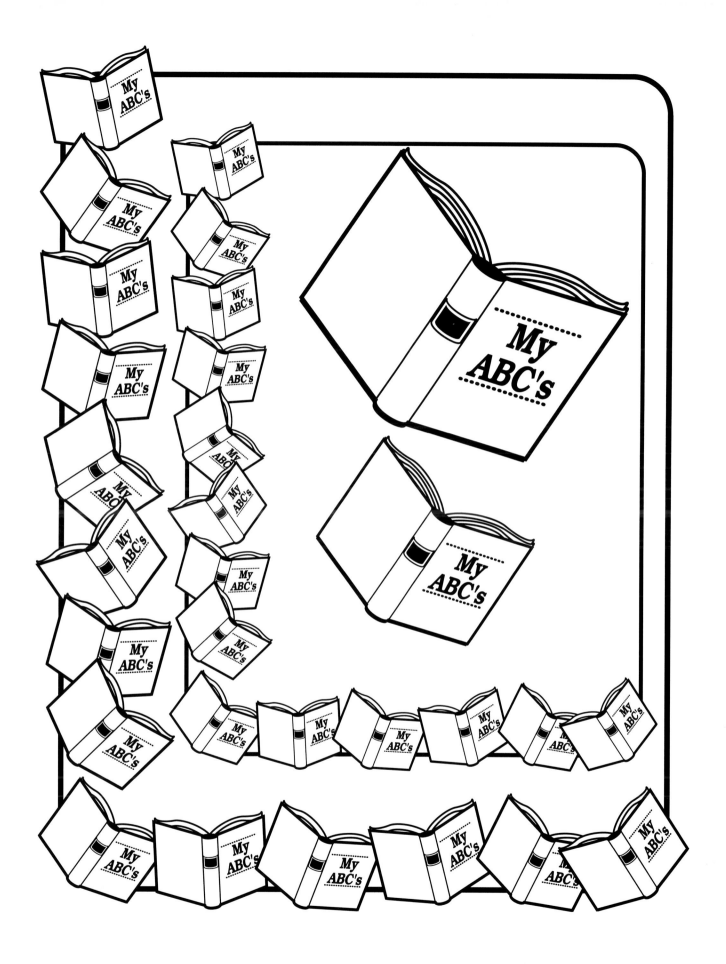

Ghost Stories

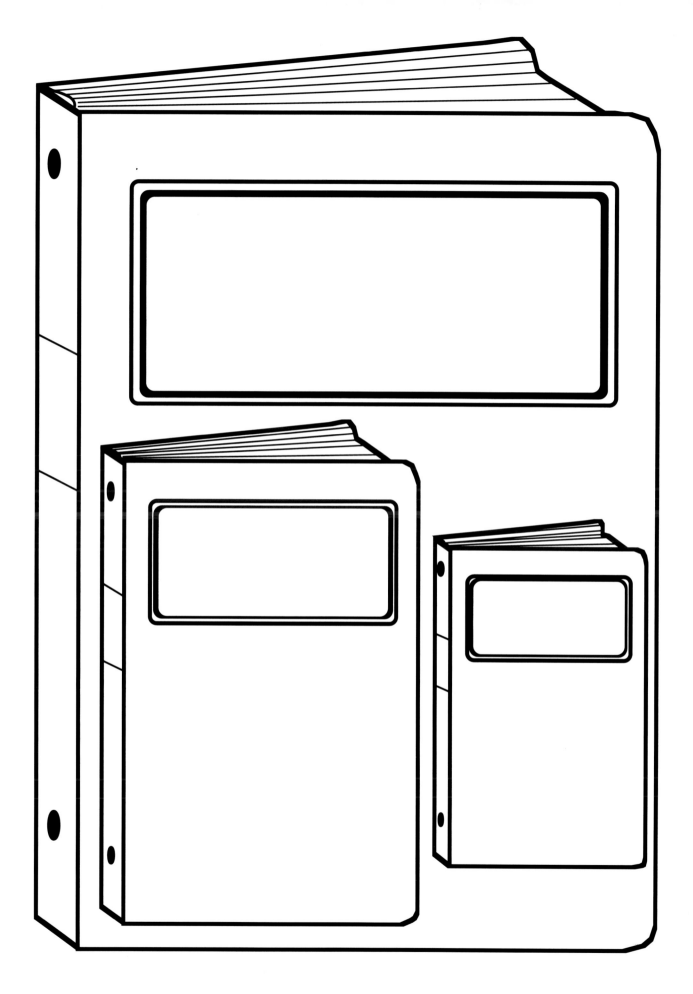

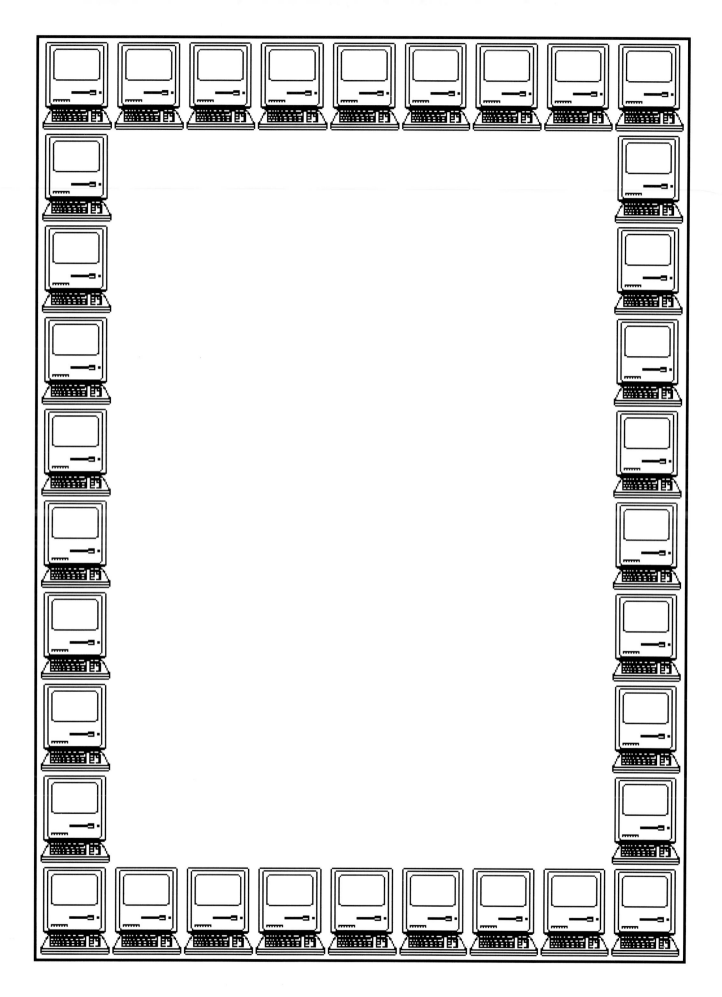

Computer Club!

Computer Club!

Films & Filmstrips

Films & Filmstrips

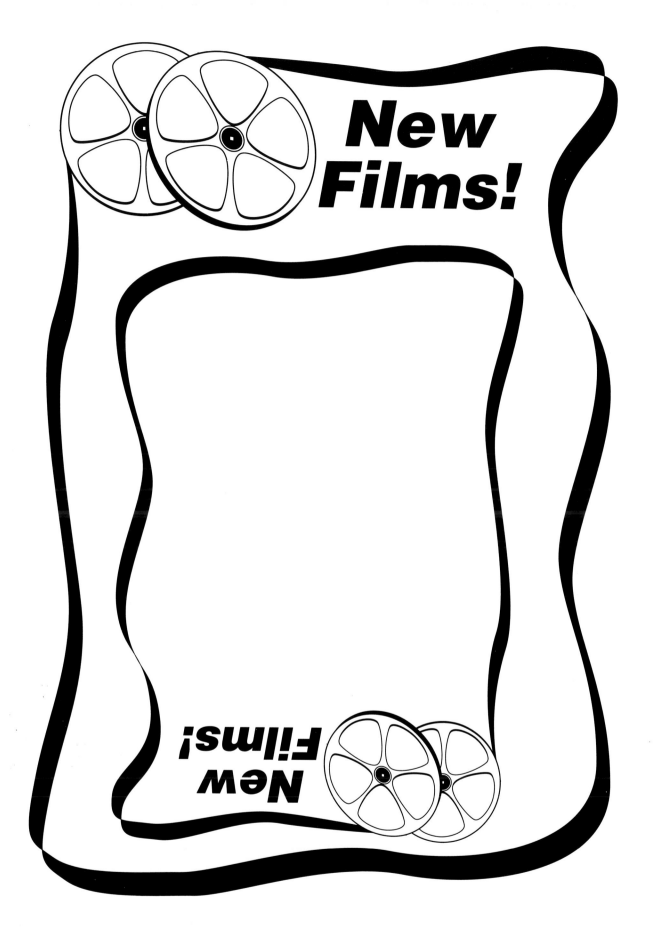

New Records!

New Records!

Section II
SIGNS & MEMOS

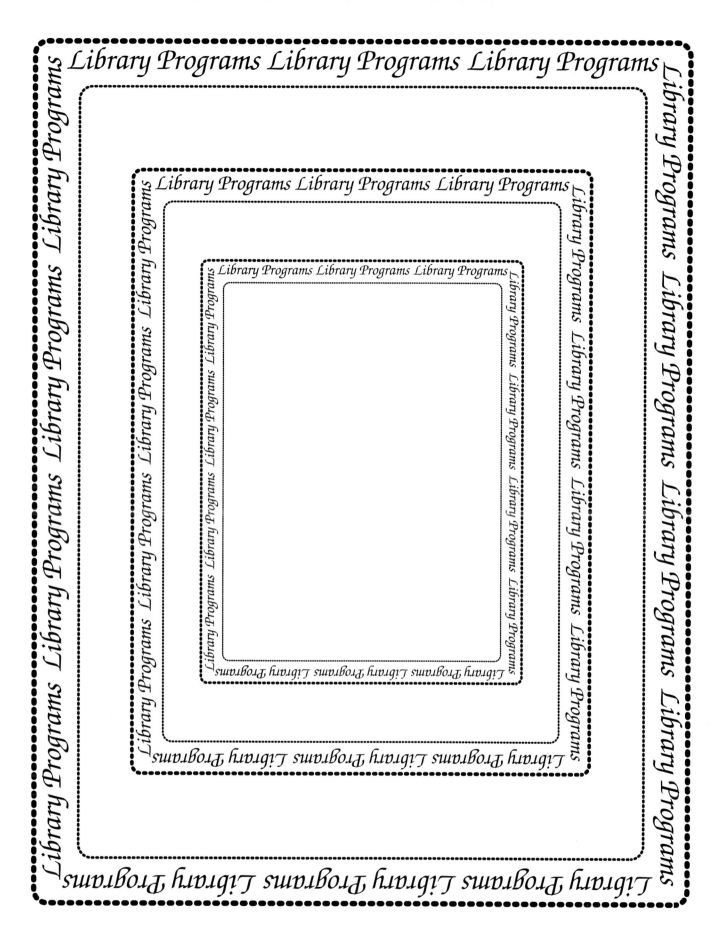

Story Hour!

Books for Children

Books for Children

Story Hour!

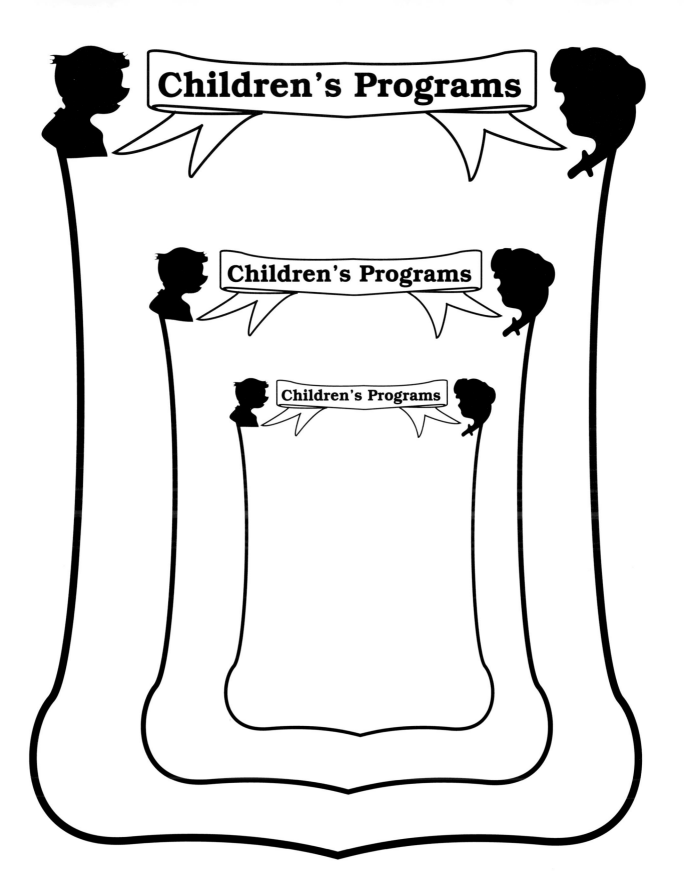

Just Say "Know"! Just Say "Know"! Just Say "Know"!

Just Say "Know"! Just Say "Know"! Just Say "Know"!

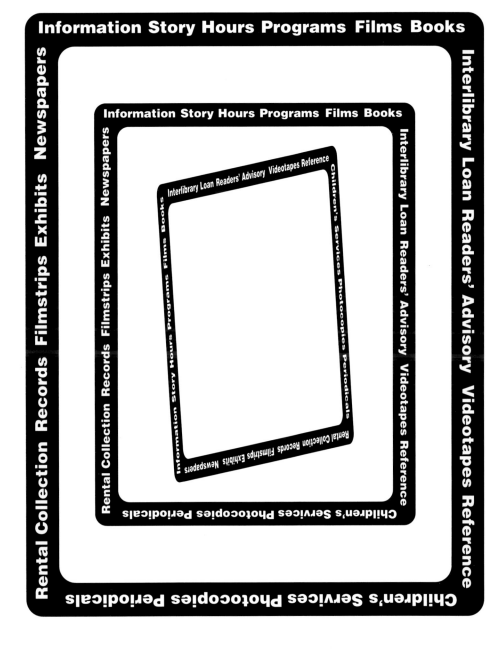

21

HOLIDAY HOURS

HOLIDAY HOURS

HOLIDAY HOURS

Large-Print Books

Large-Print Books

Large-Print Books

Large-Print Books

New On The Shelf

New On The Shelf

New On The Shelf

NEWSPAPERS!

NEWSPAPERS!

It's For You!
Telephone
Reference Service

It's For You!
Telephone Reference Service

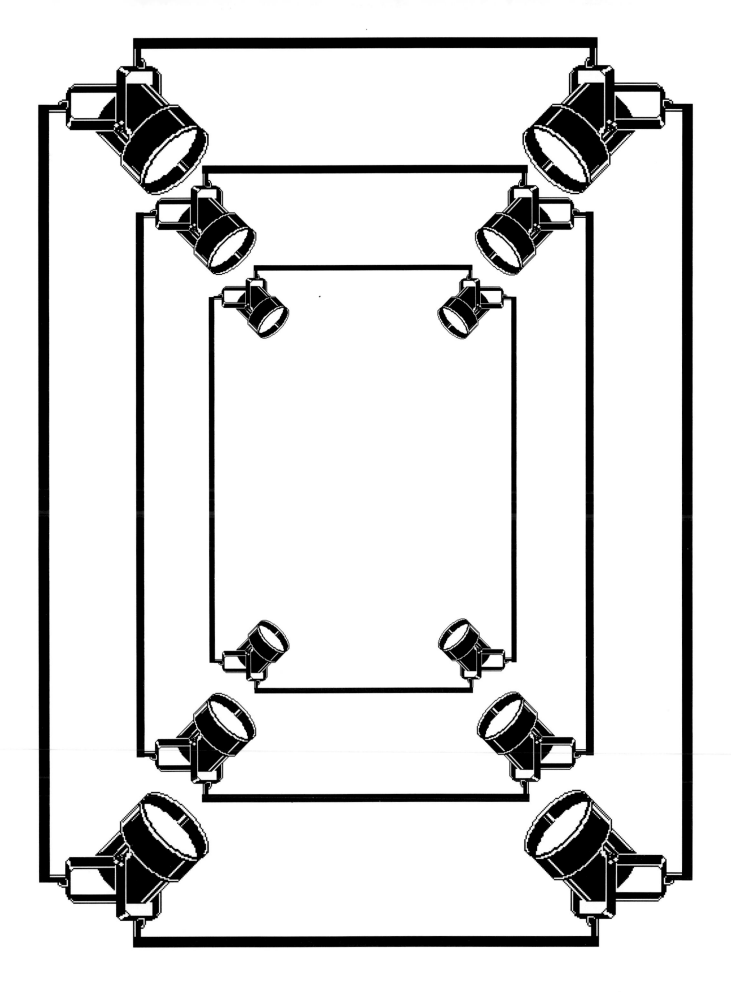

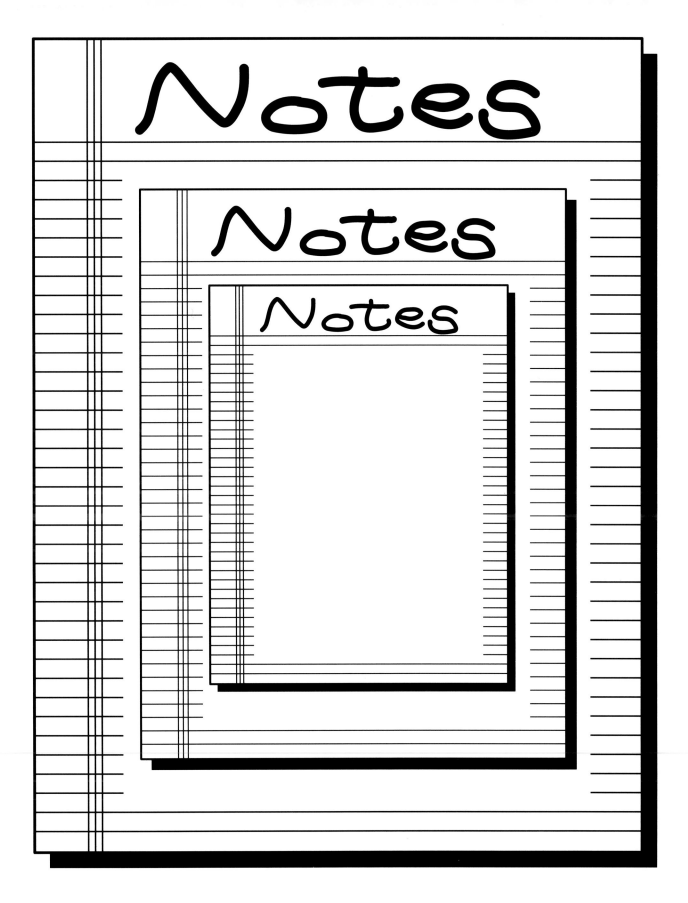

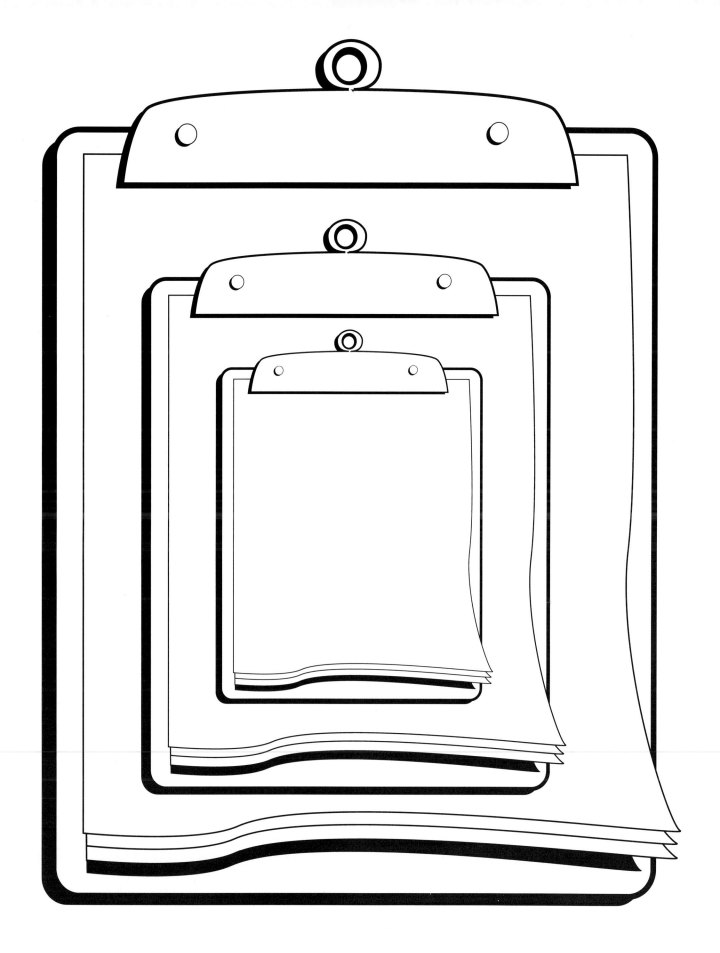

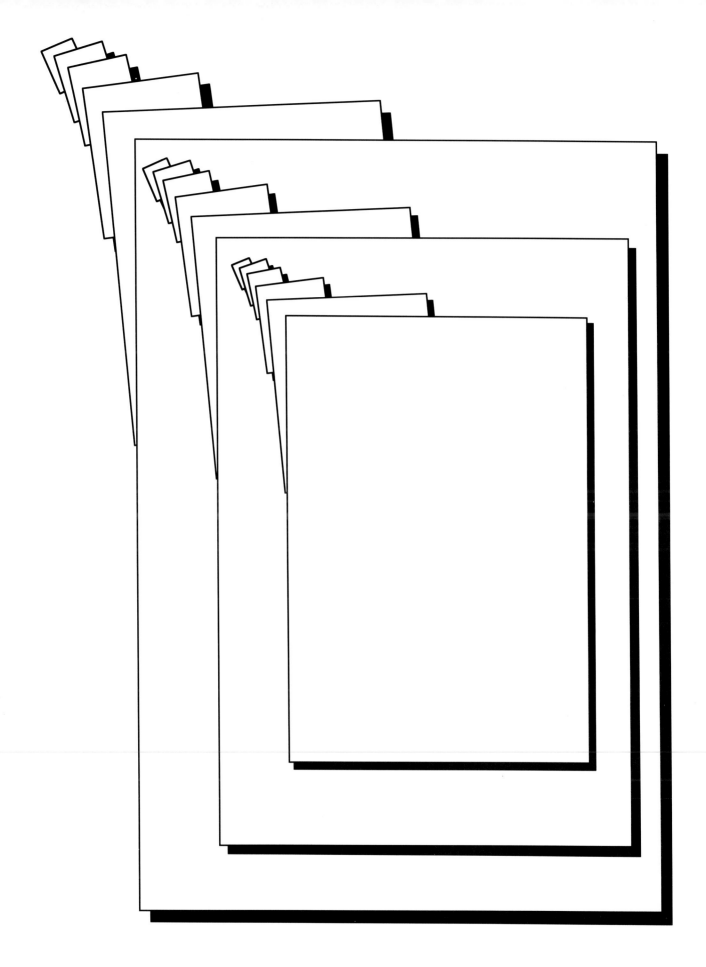

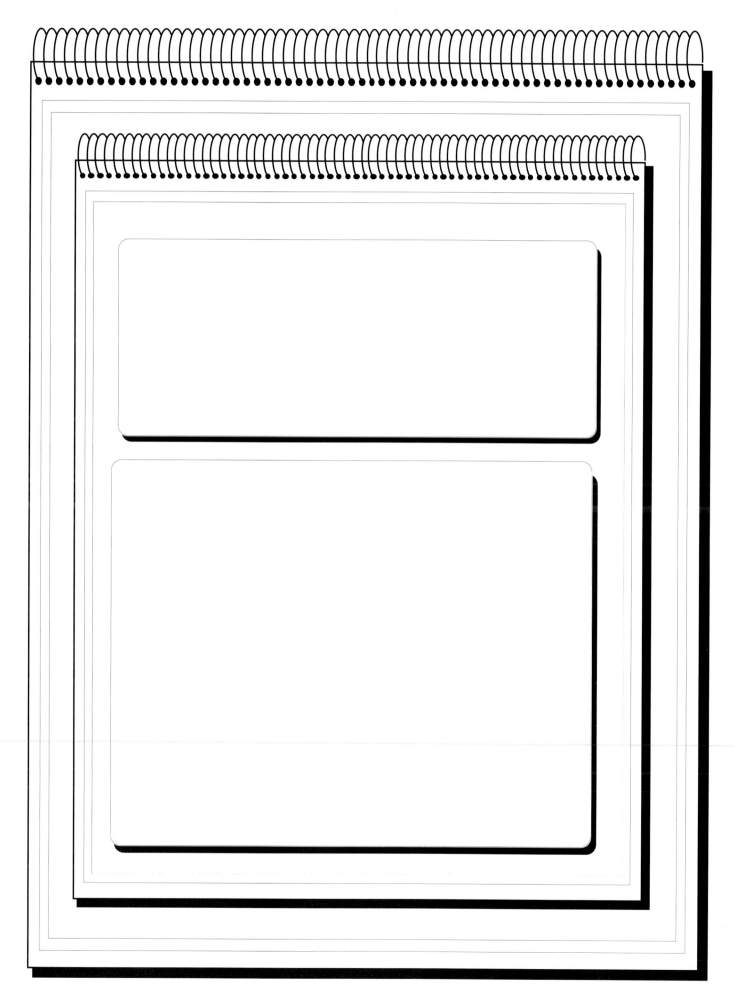

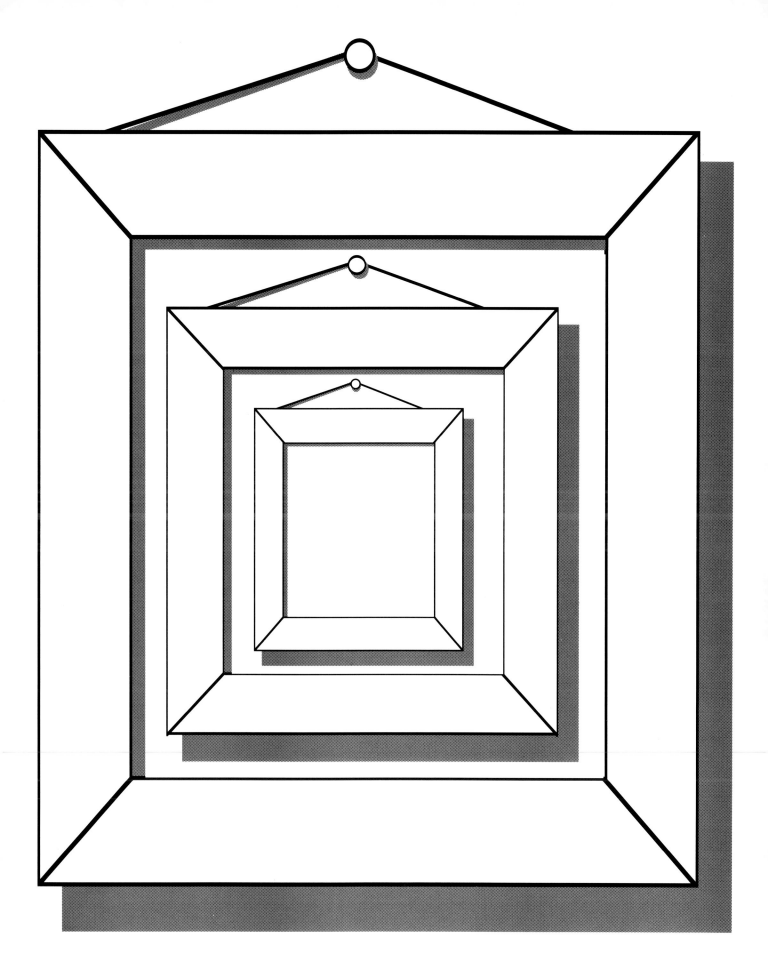

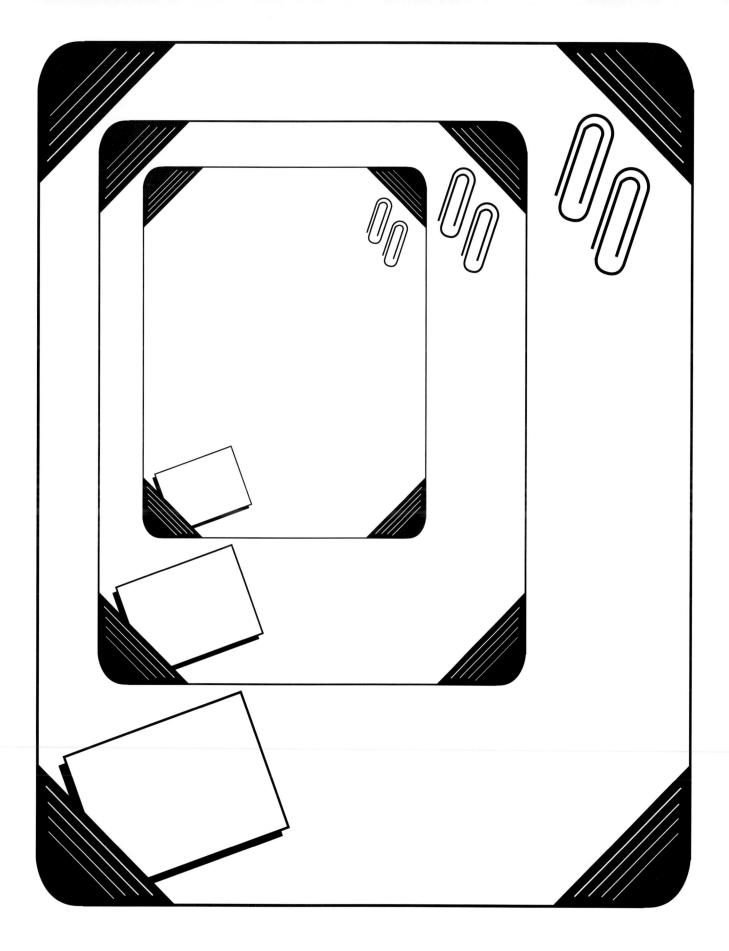

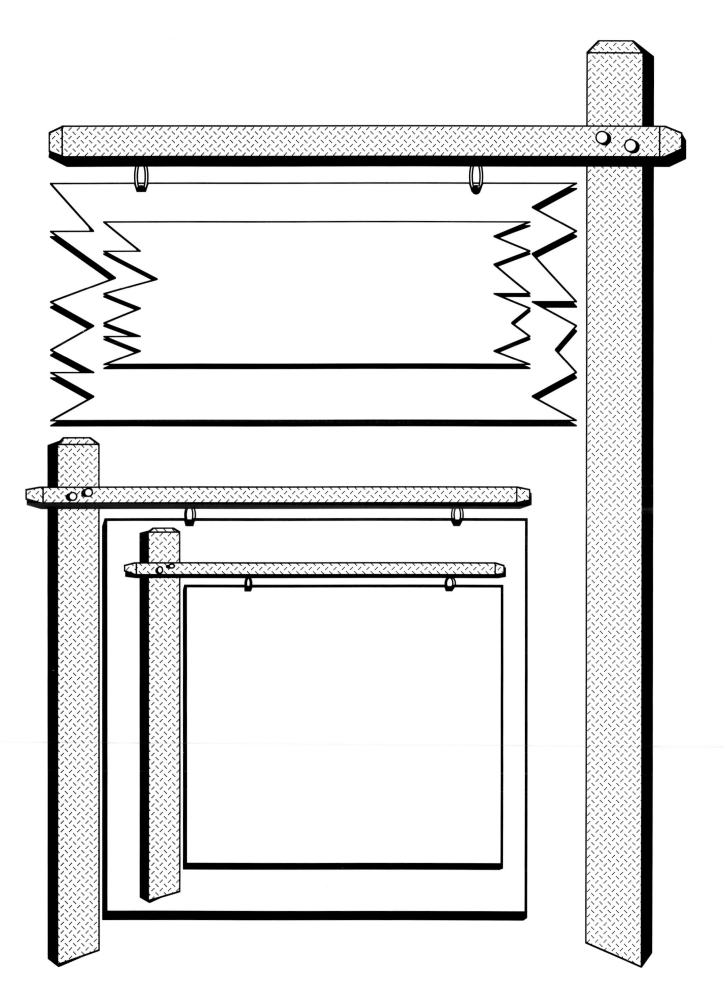

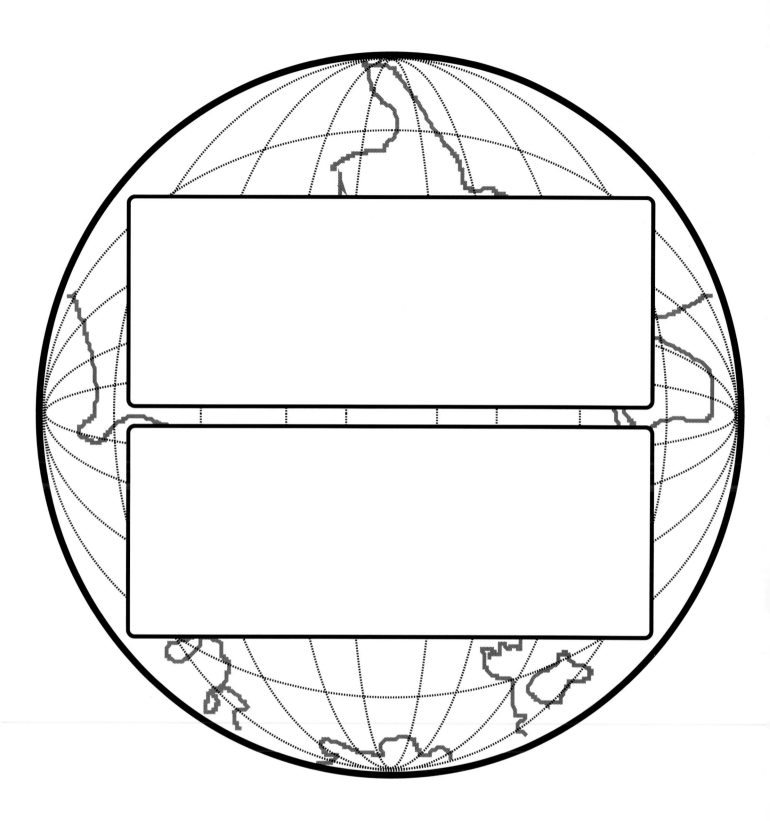

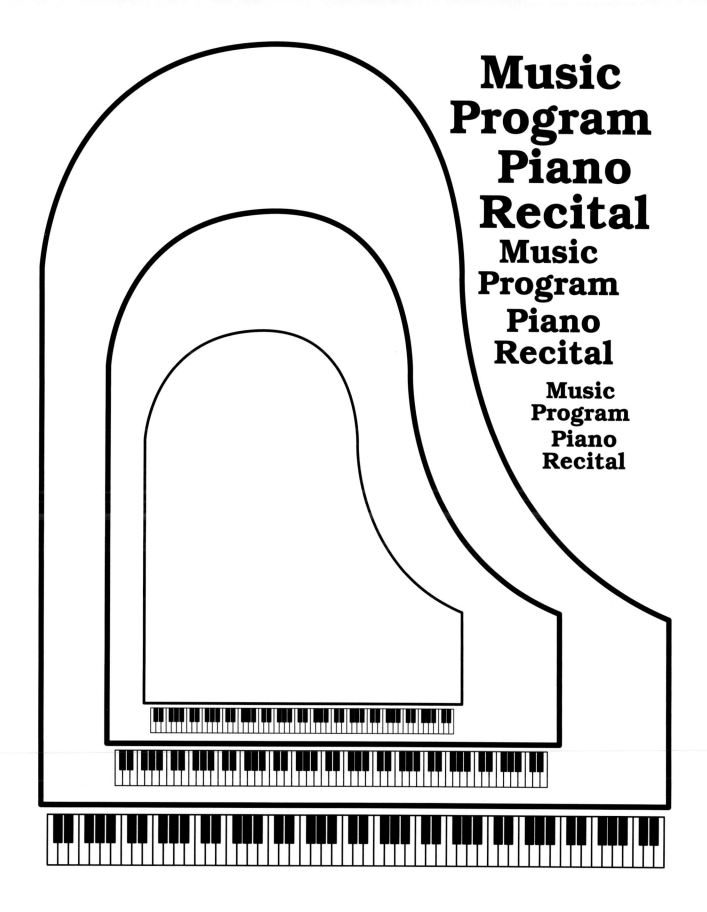

Music
Program
Piano
Recital
Music
Program
Piano
Recital
Music
Program
Piano
Recital

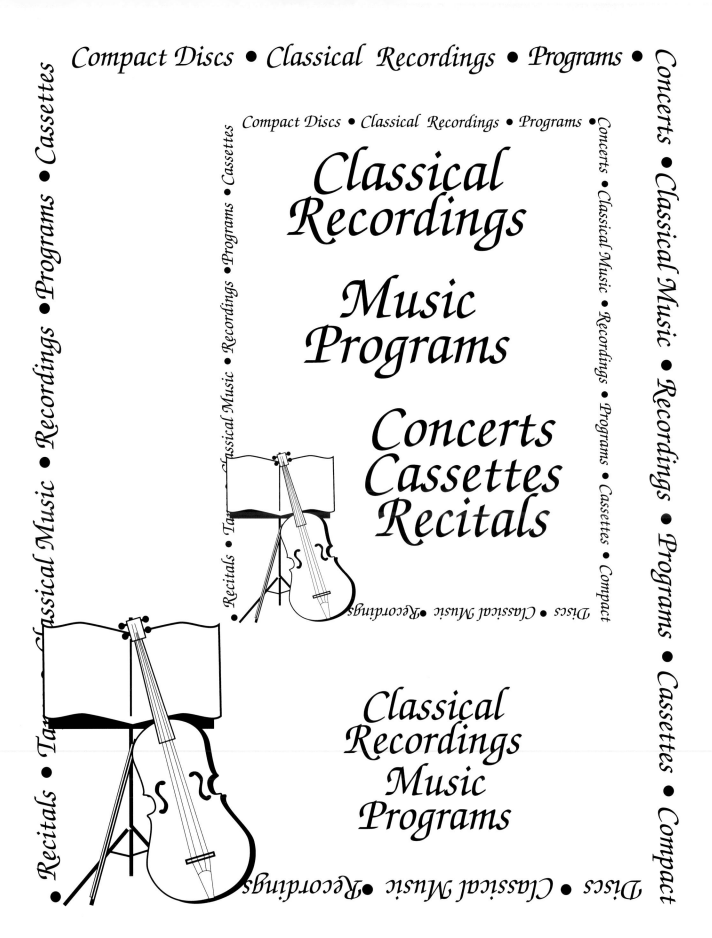

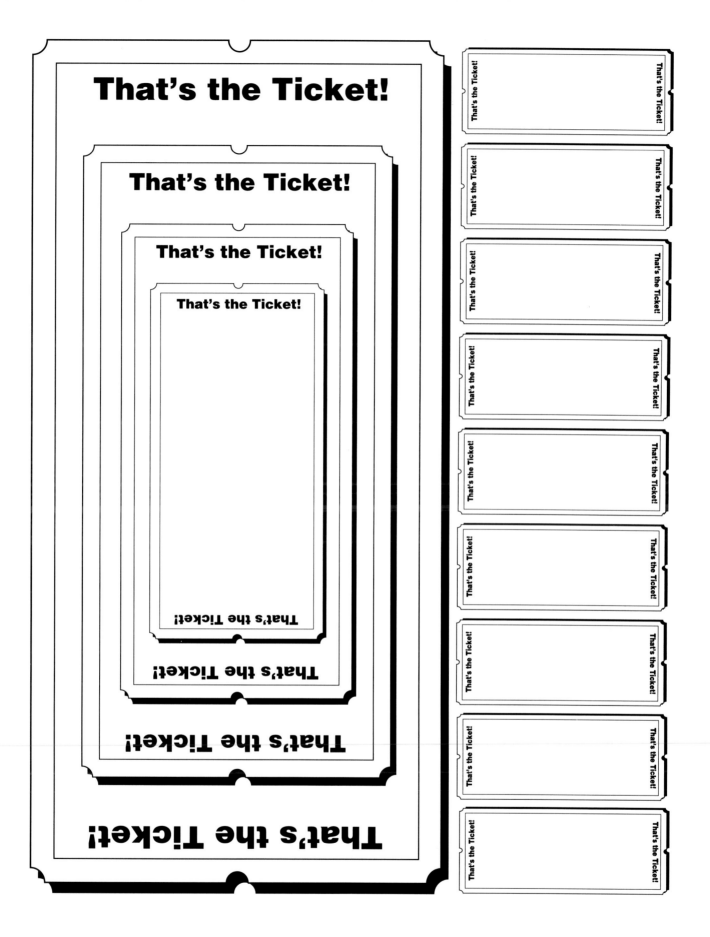

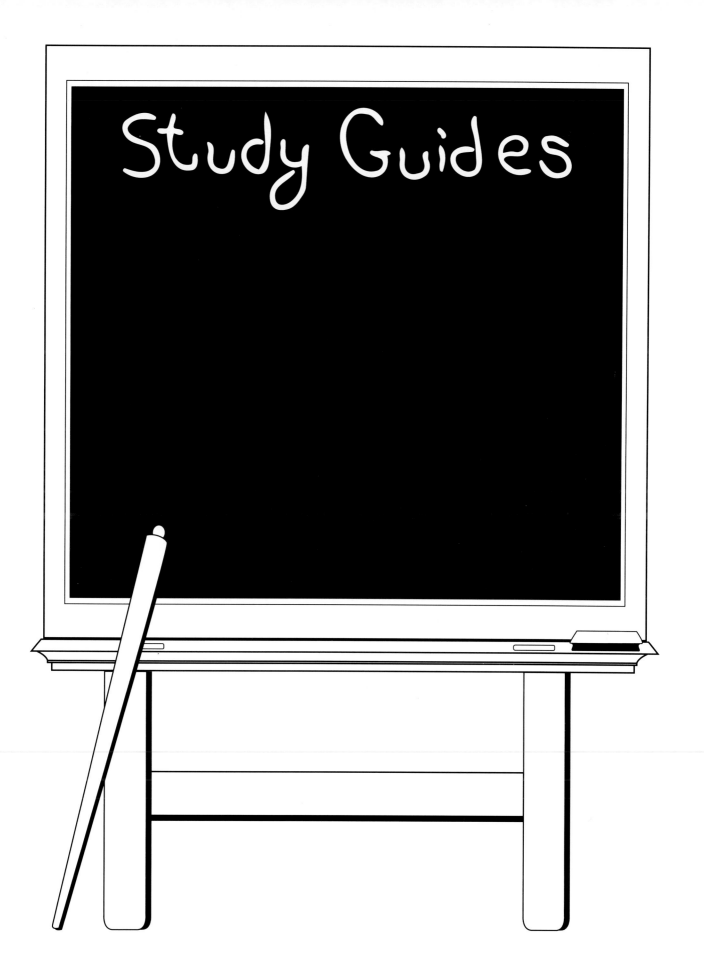

SCHEDULE
MONDAY TUESDAY WEDNESDAY THURSDAY
FRIDAY SATURDAY SUNDAY

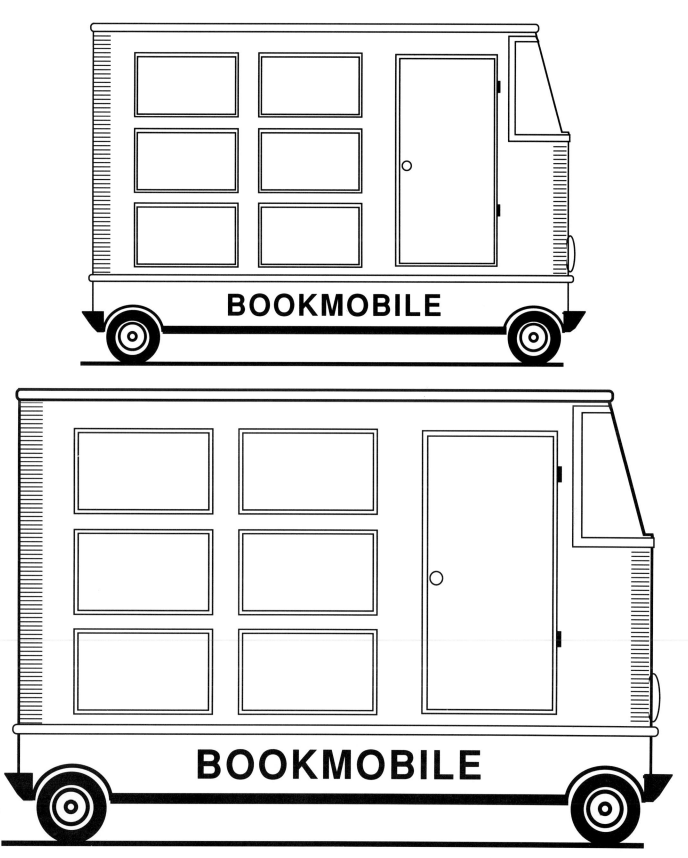

BOOKMOBILE

BOOKMOBILE

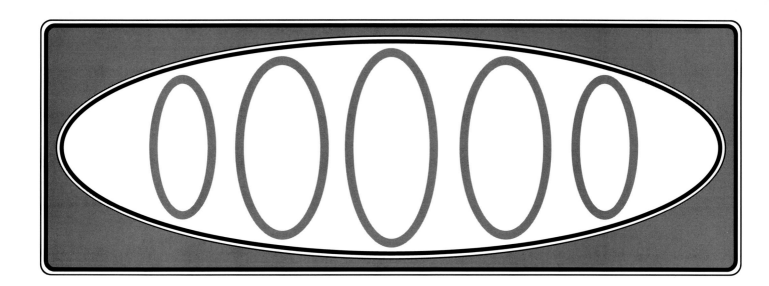

Second Fold

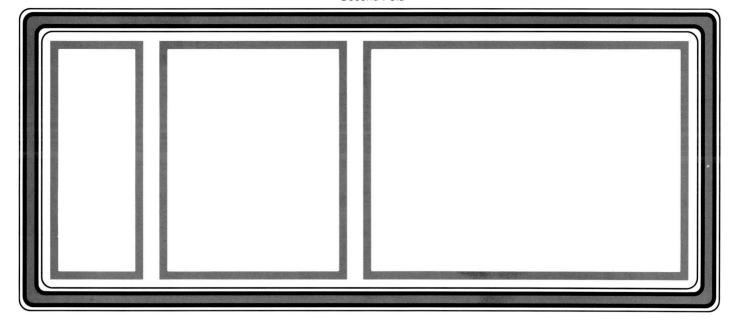

First Fold

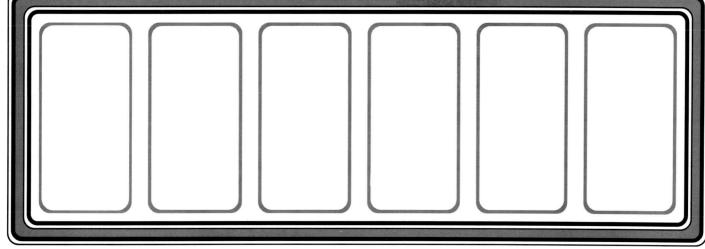

42

The borders shown here and on the previous page are designed to be used as a 6 page, 8 1/2" x 11" tri-fold brochure. The smaller ovals and rectangles can be used to frame heads or sub-heads, as well as utilized to highlight copy blocks which you would like to emphasize (i.e., hours of opening, ticket prices, etc.).

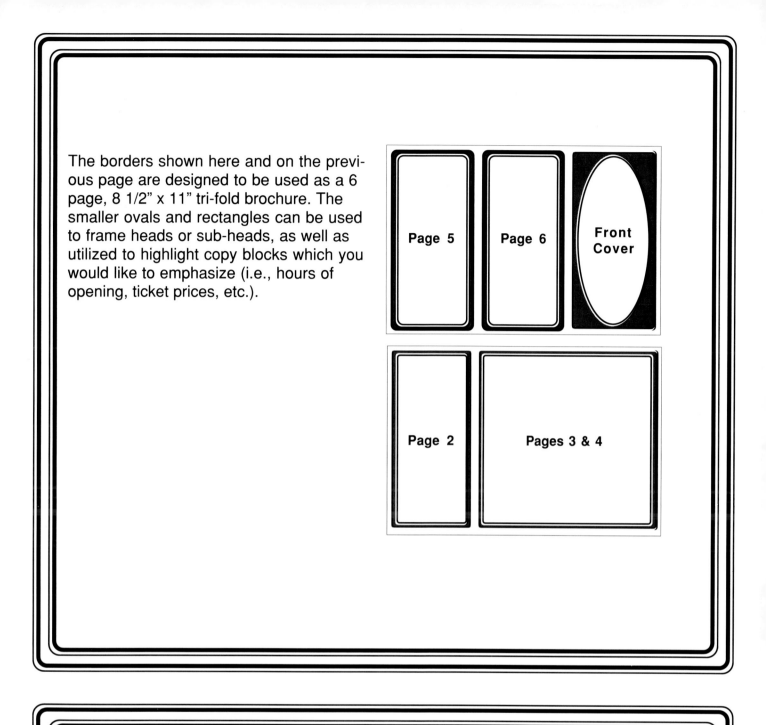

Section III
HOLIDAYS

1989   1990

1991   1992
1993   1994

Happy New Year!
Happy New Year!
Happy New Year!

1995   1996
1997   1998

1989   1990

**Happy
St. Patrick's Day!**

**Happy
St. Patrick's Day!**

*Looking over a
4-leaf clover*

Irish Authors

*Jewels from
the
Emerald Isle*

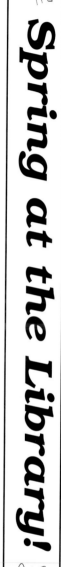

Spring at the Library!

Spring at the Library!

Spring at the Library!

Spring at the Library!

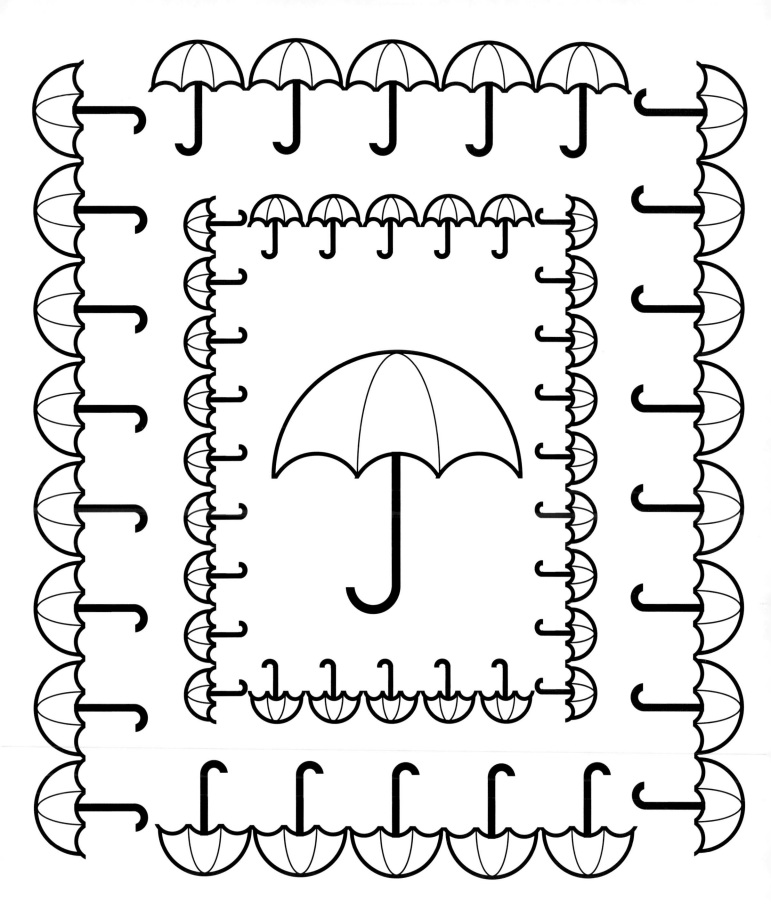

51

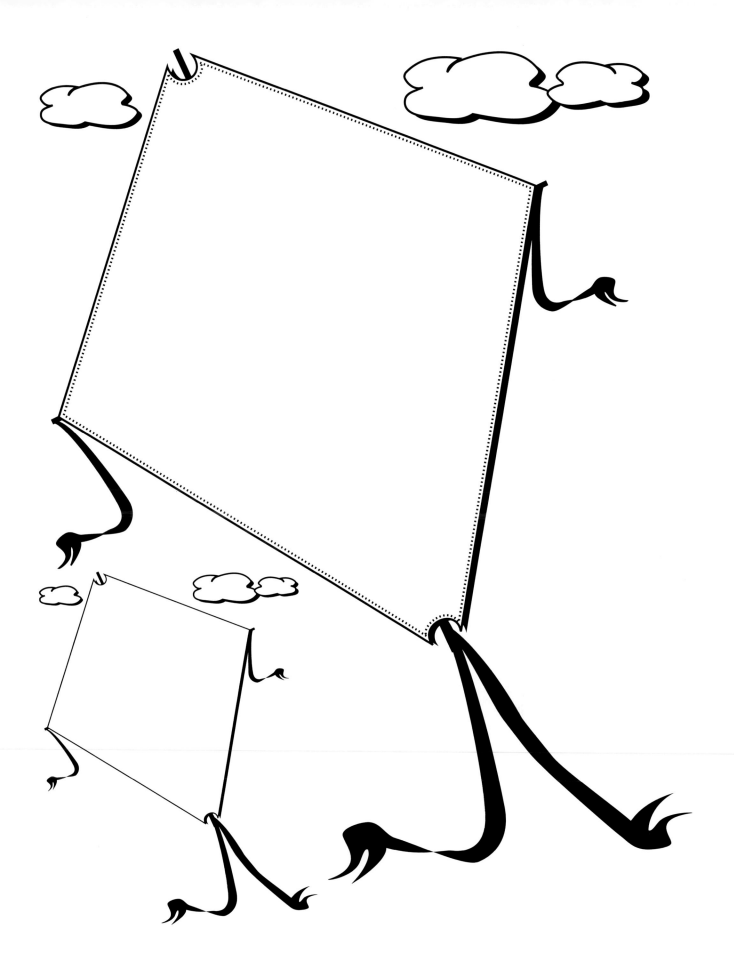

54

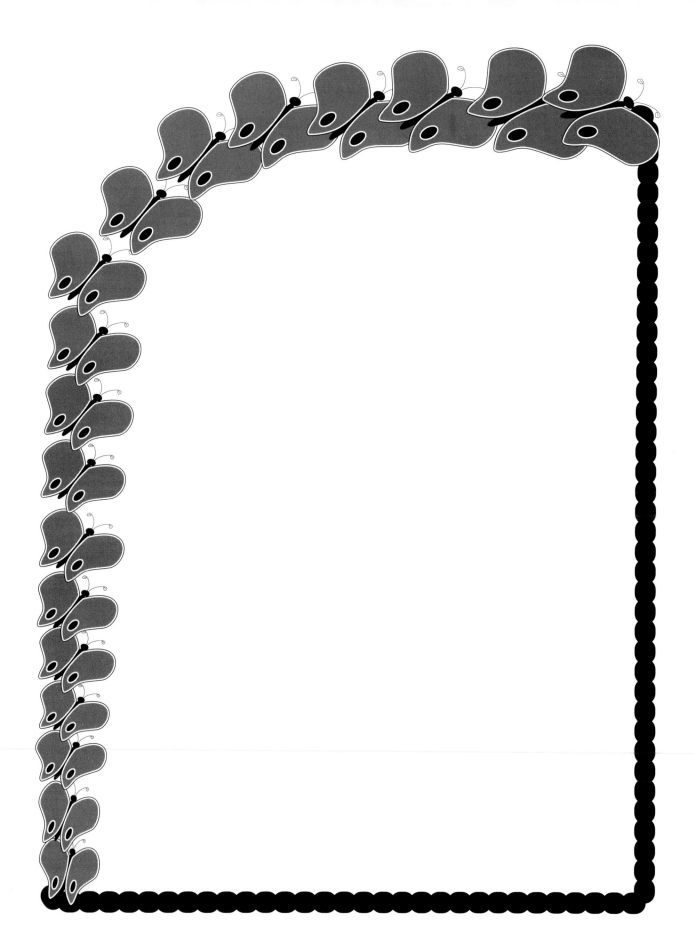

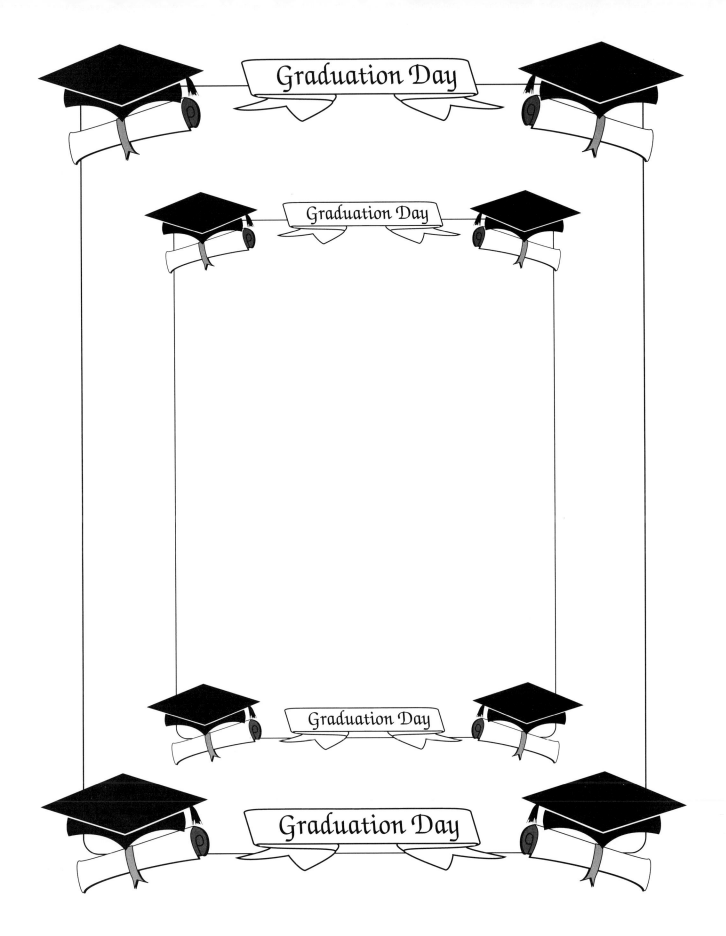

Graduation Day

Graduation Day

Graduation Day

Graduation Day

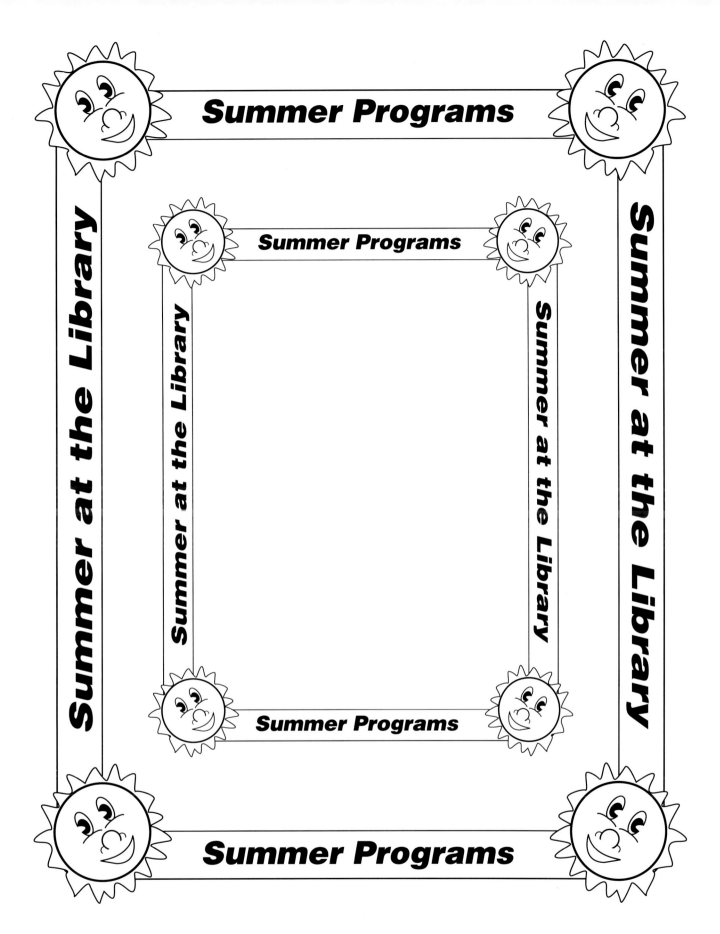

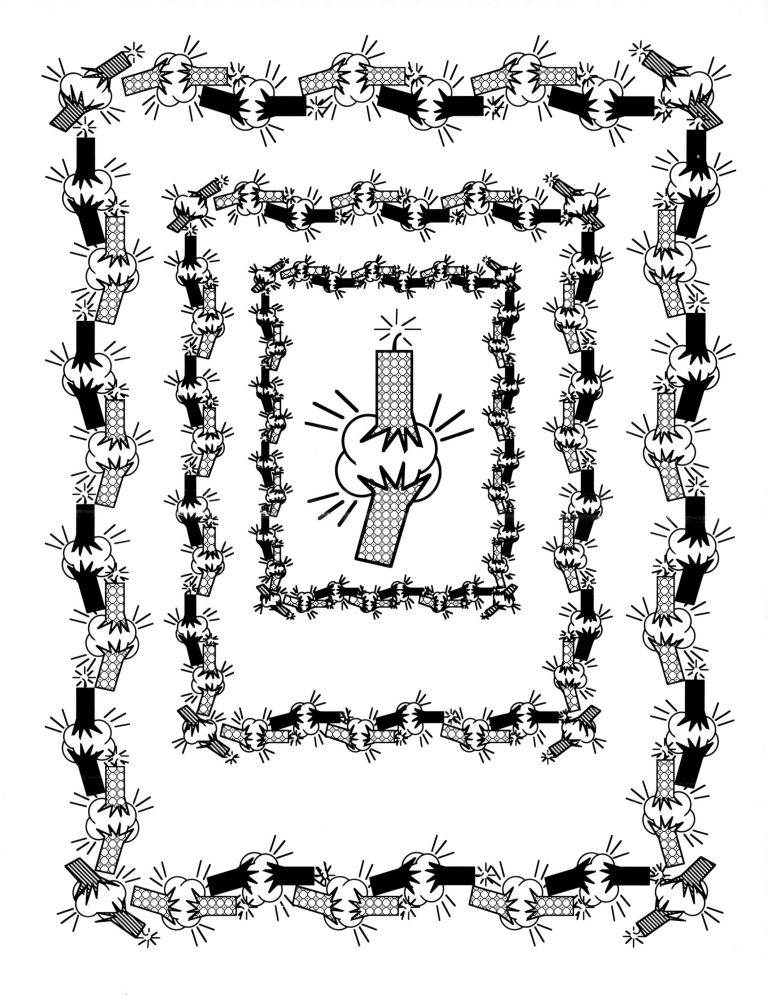

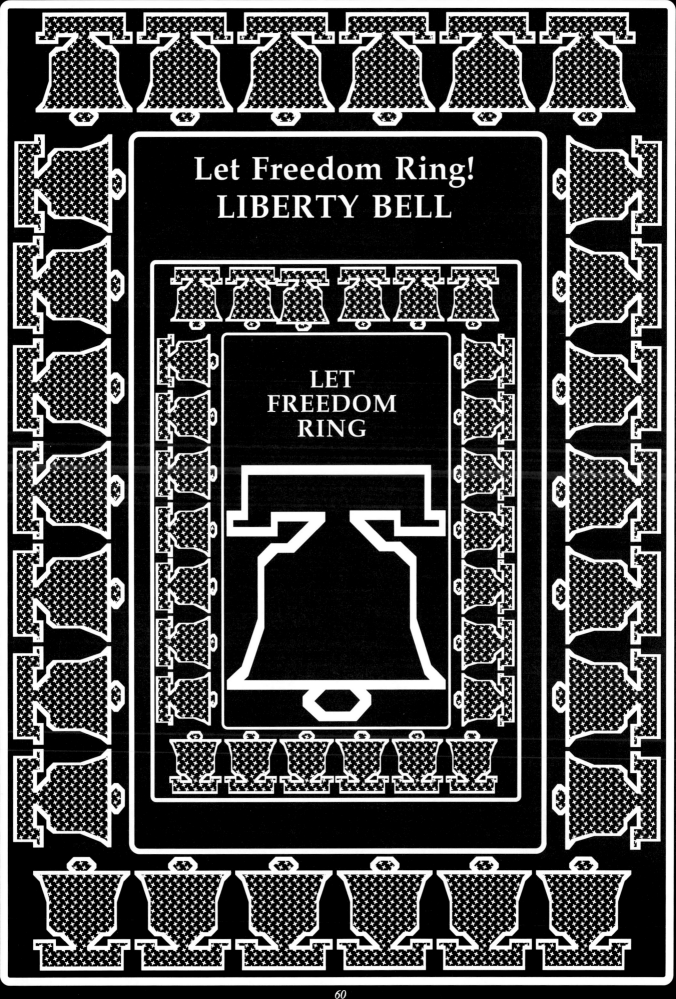

Let Freedom Ring!
LIBERTY BELL

LET FREEDOM RING

Fall at the Library

WINTER ACTIVITIES at the Library!

WINTER ACTIVITIES at the Library!

WINTER ACTIVITIES at the Library!

WINTER ACTIVITIES at the Library!

Happy Chanukah!

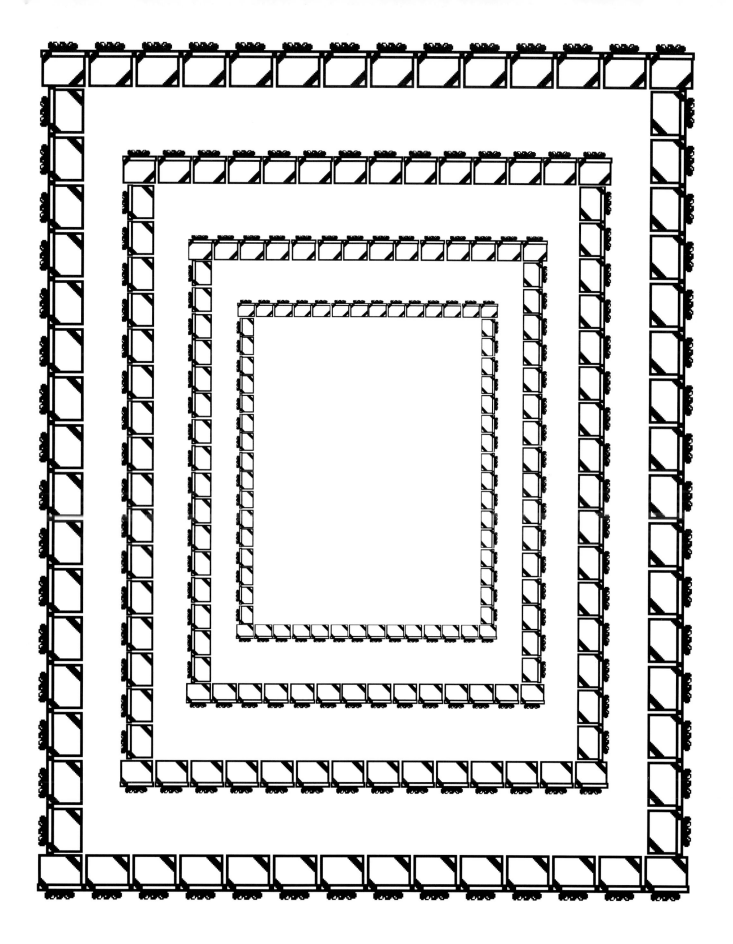

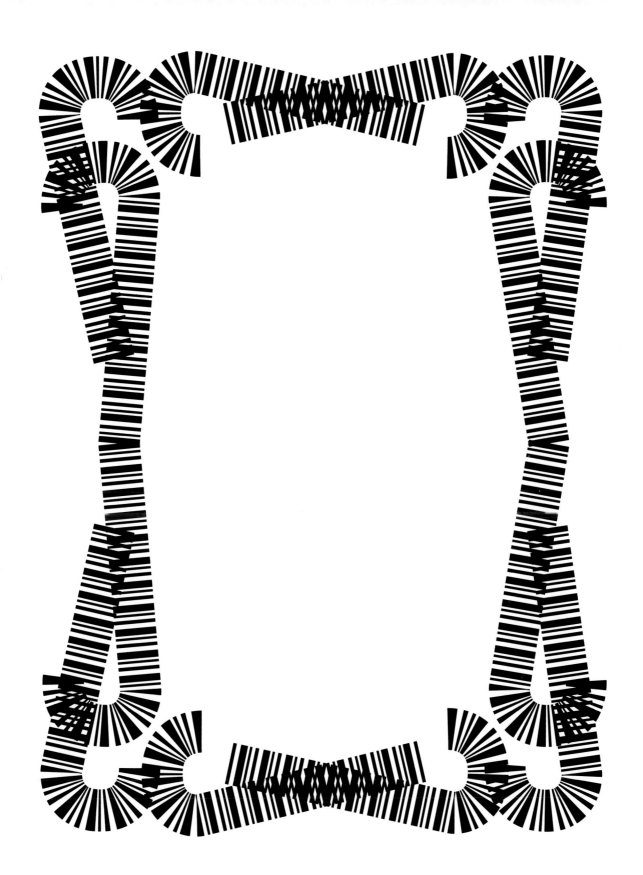

Section IV
ART

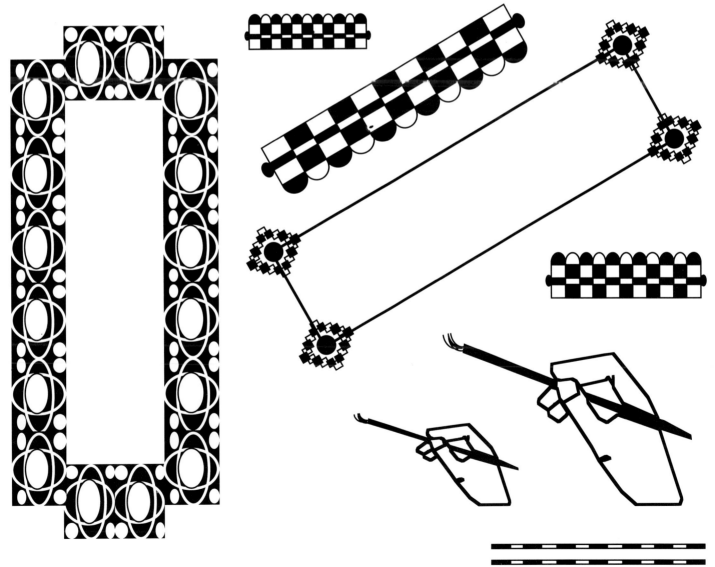

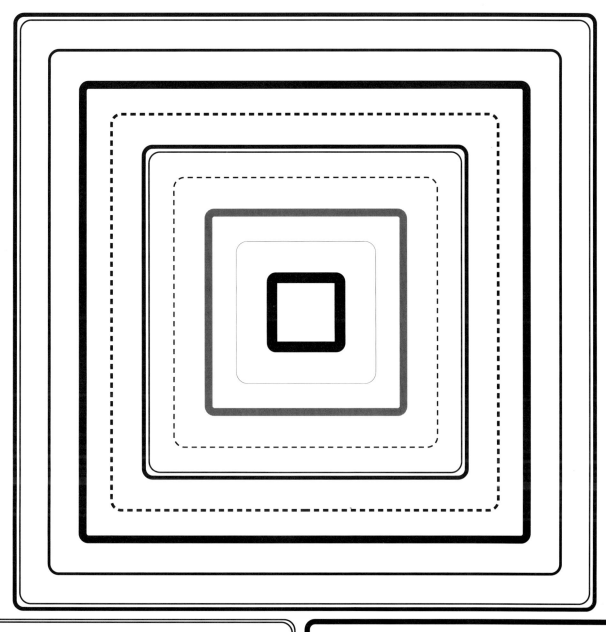

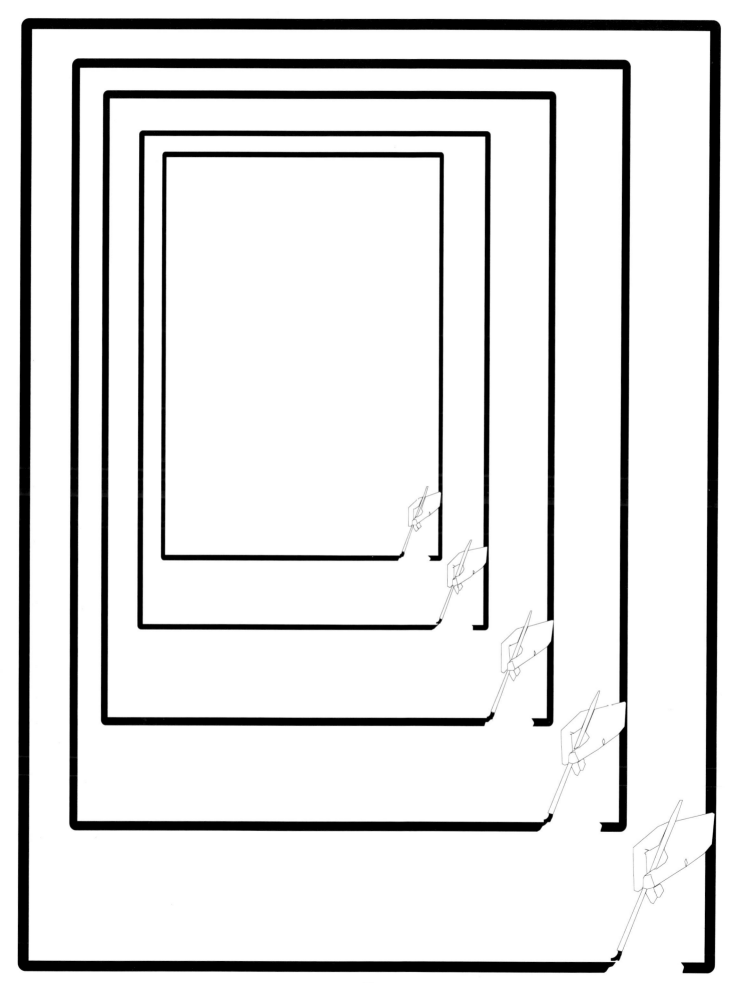

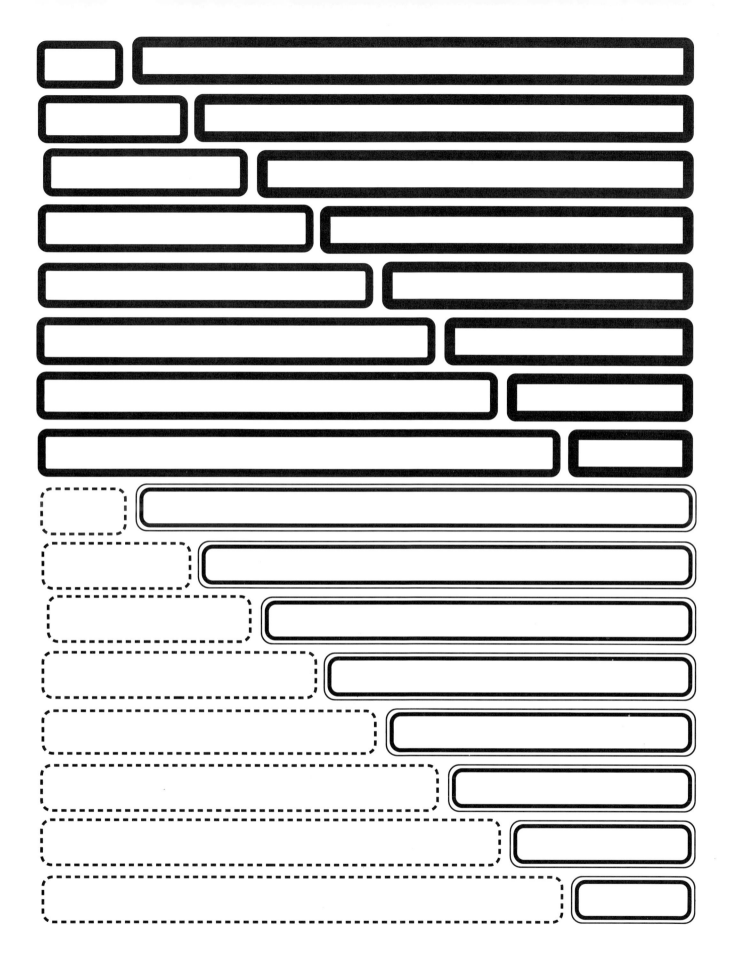

92

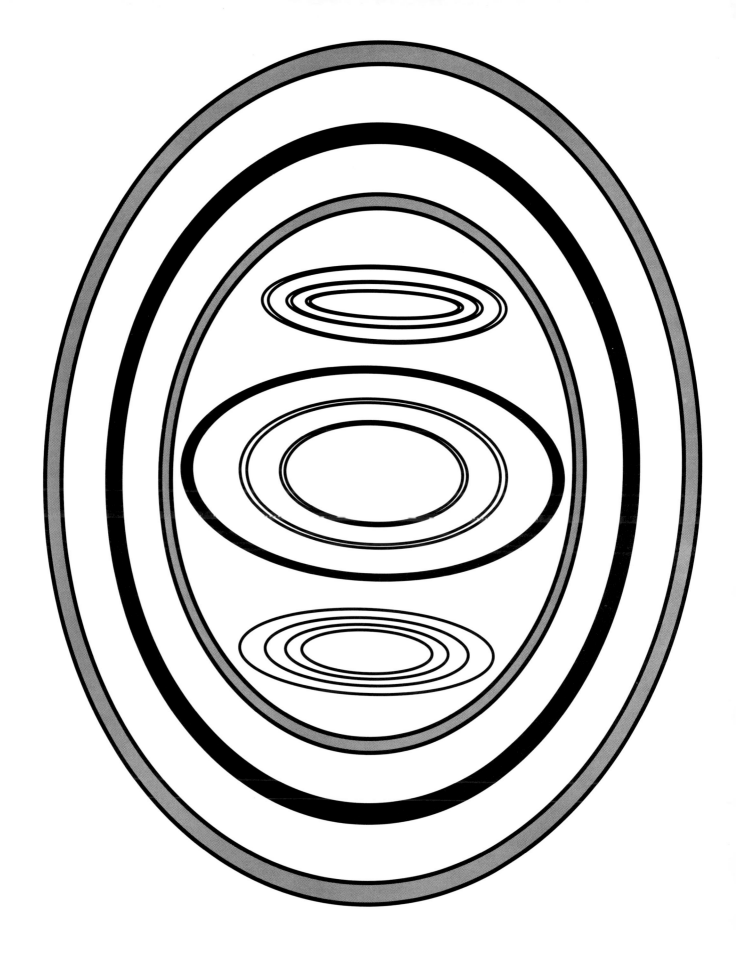

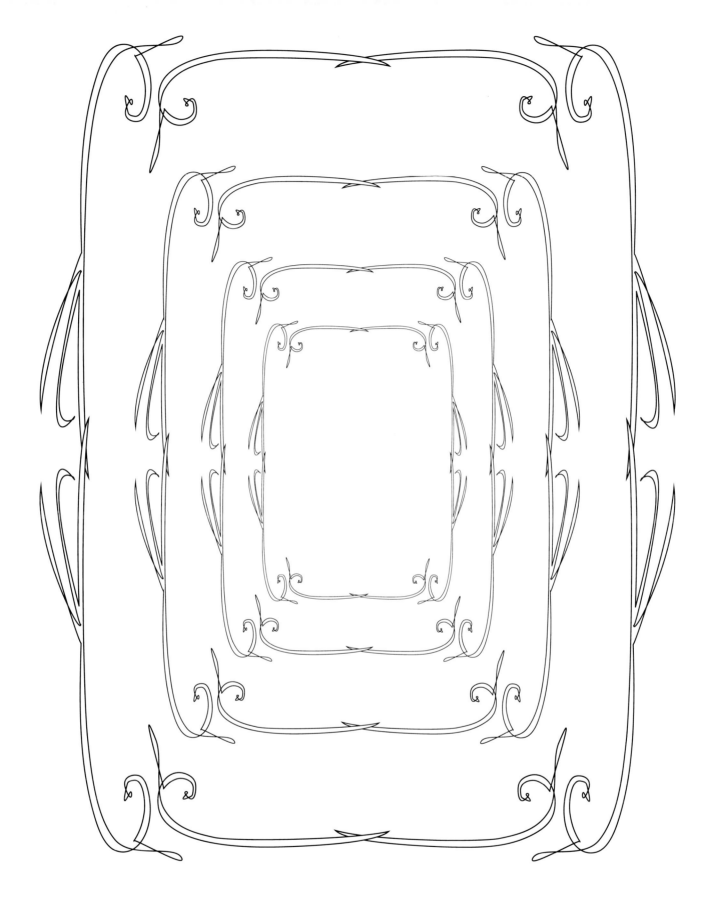

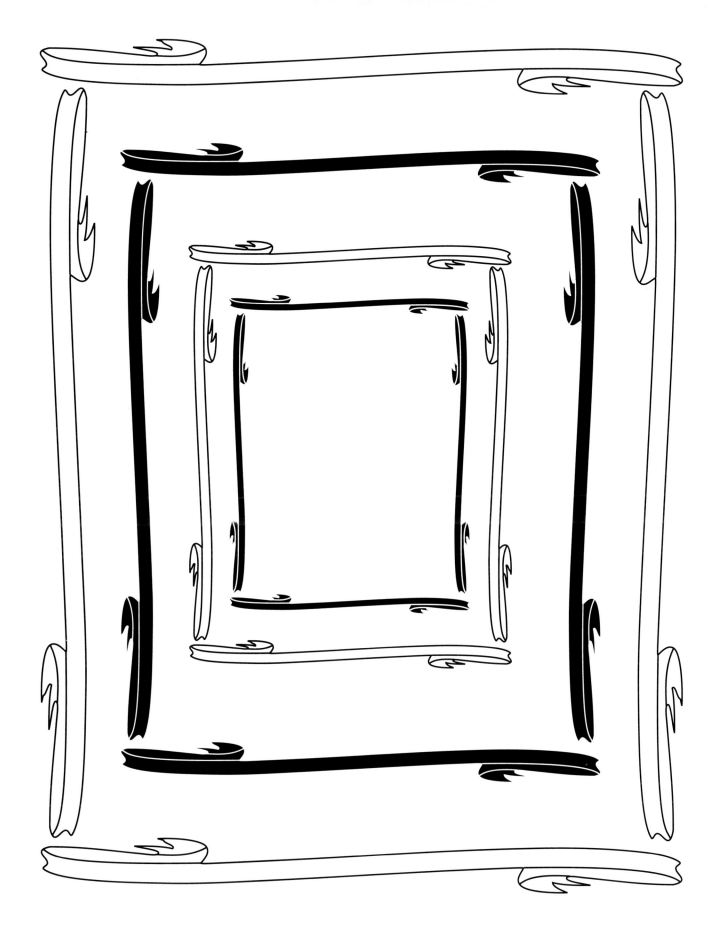

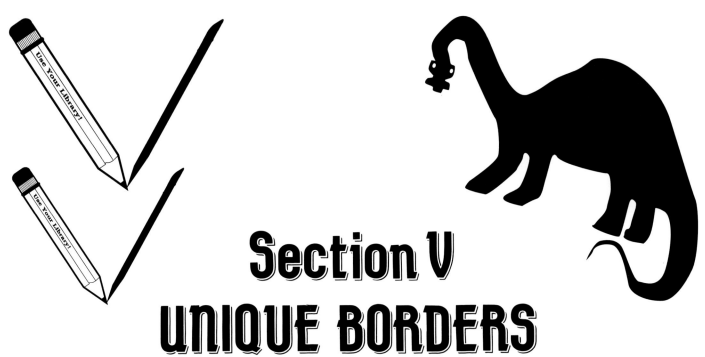

Section V
UNIQUE BORDERS

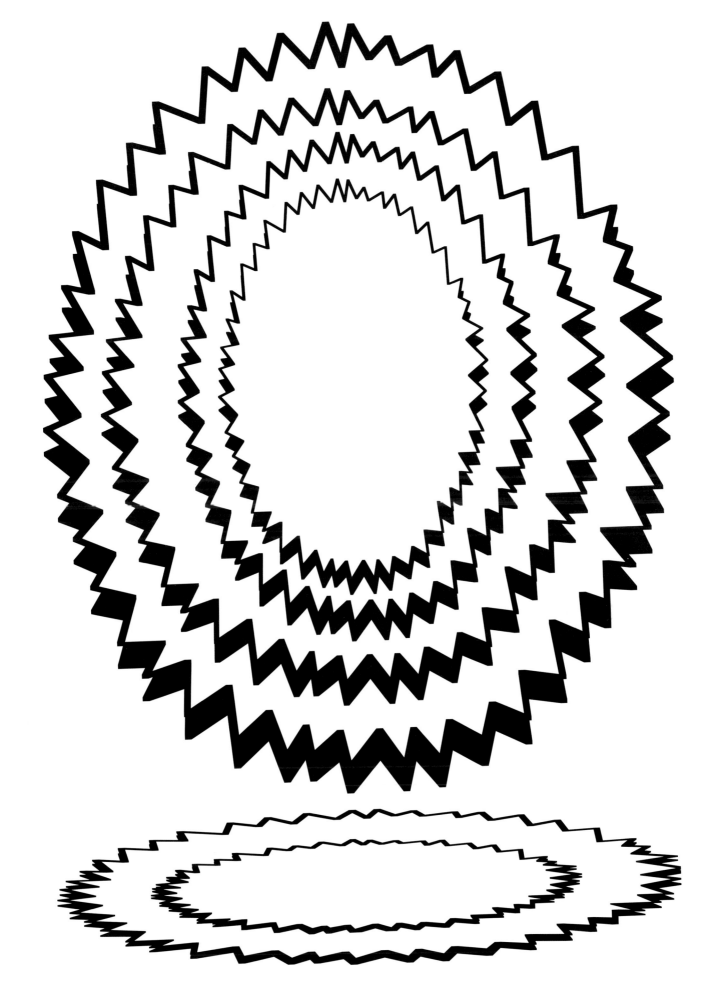

101

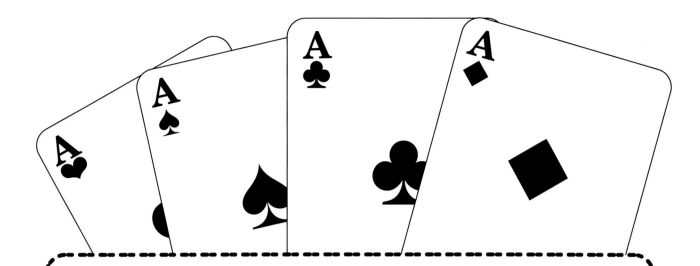

A Winning Hand!
Four of a Kind!

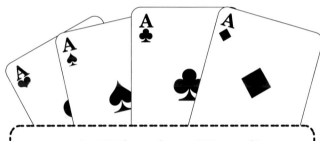

A Winning Hand!
Four of a Kind!

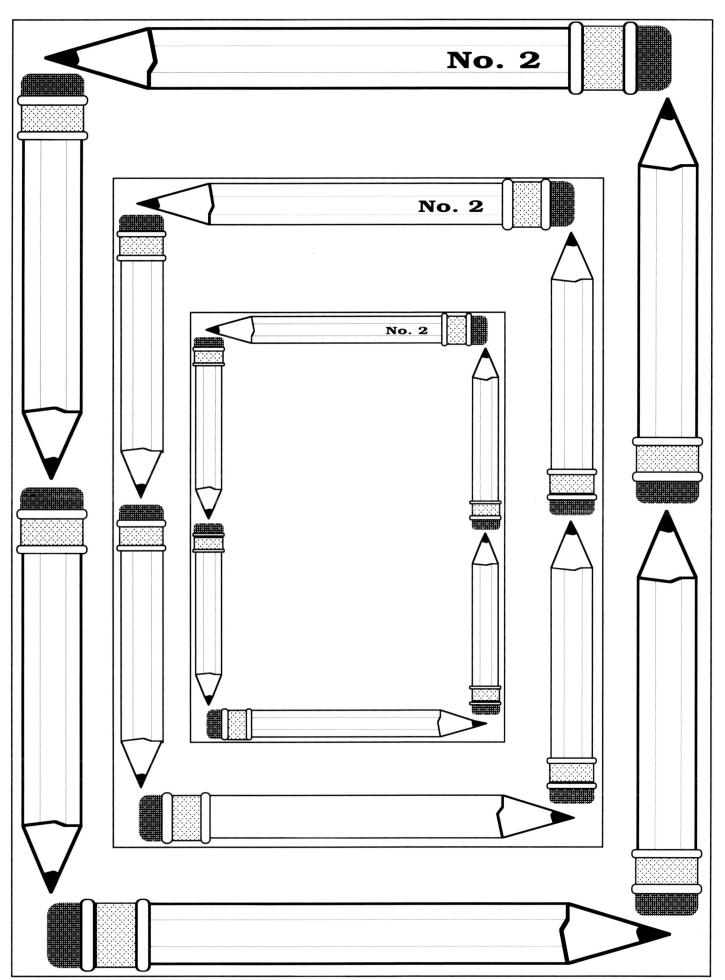

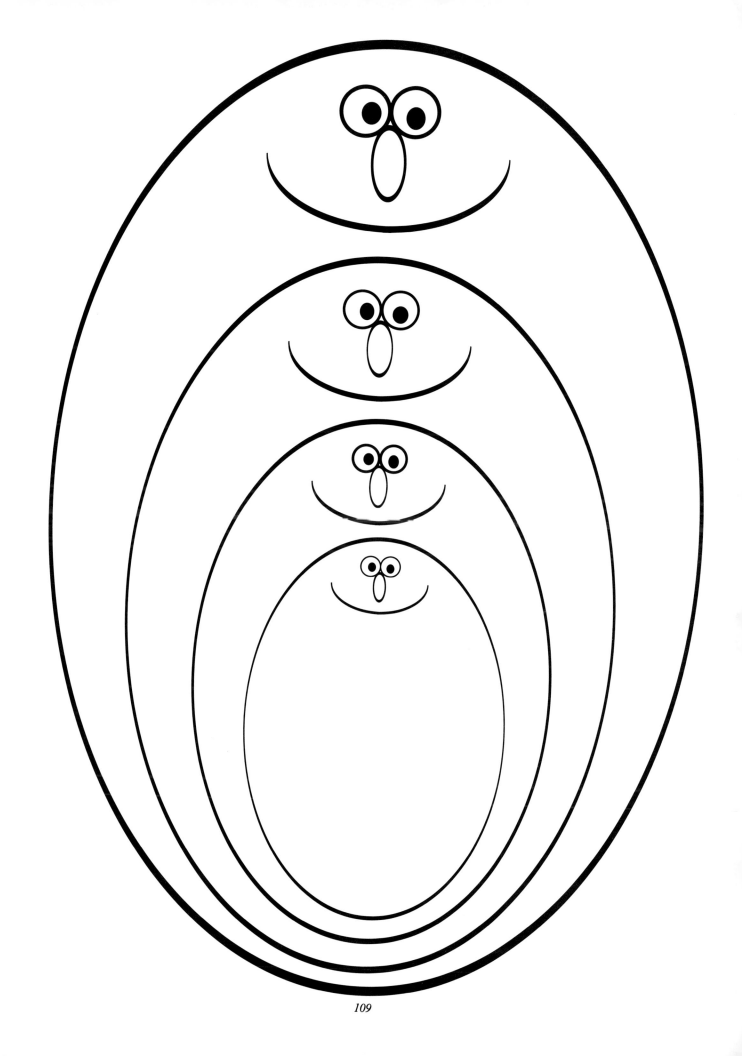

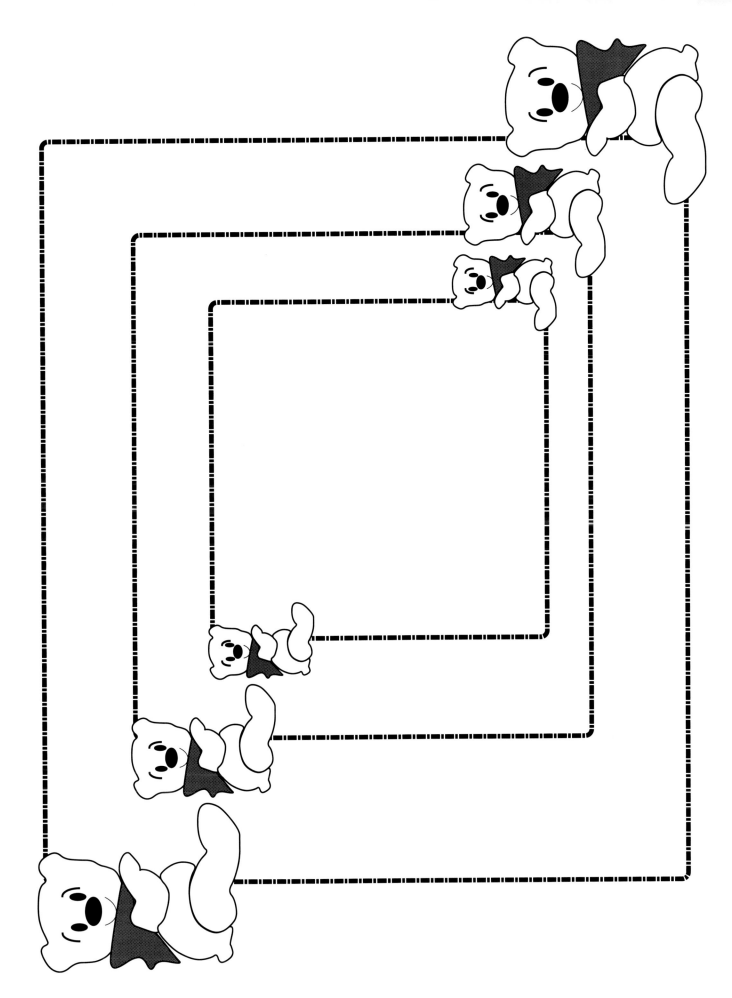

Section VI
TREASURY

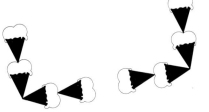

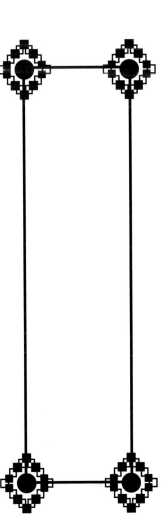

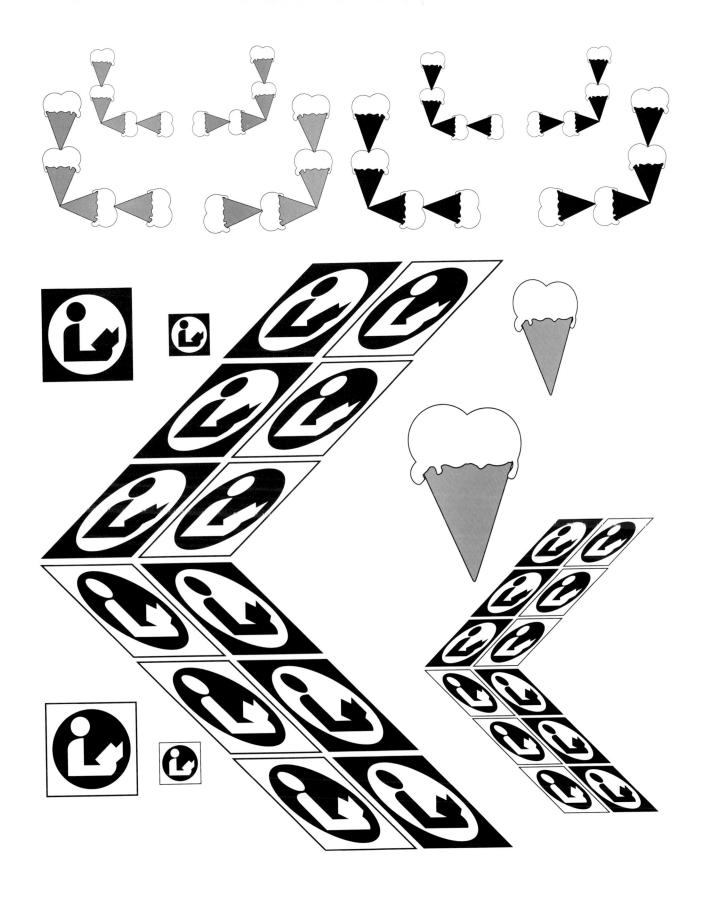

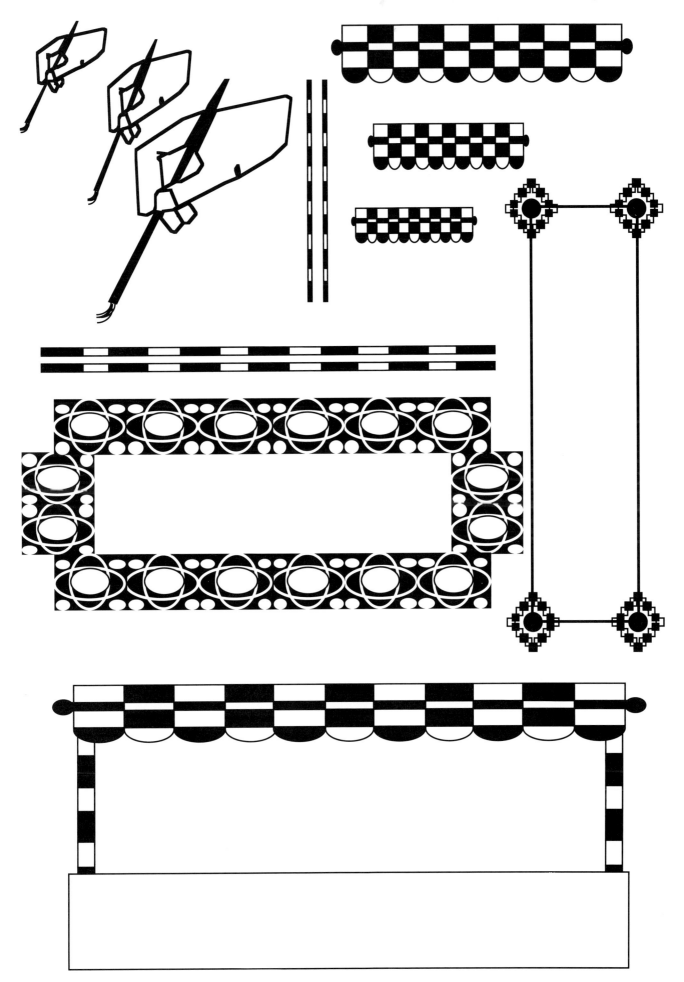

INDEX

Alphabet, 74
Animals
    Bunny, 117
    Bunny in hat, 20
    Butterflies, 55, 118
    Dinosaurs, 102, 124
    Teddy bears, 111
Audiovisual
    Cello on stand, 38
    Films/filmstrips, 10
    New films, 11
    New records, 12
    Piano, 37, 115
Axe, 46, 122
Awning border, 75, 123

Bats, 63, 121
Bells, 60, 120
Bird in nest, 54
Blackboard, 40
Blotter, 33
Bookmobile, 41
Books
    Bookmobile, 41
    Books for children, 16, 114
    Bookshelf frame, 5
    Four of a kind, 104
    Ghost Stories, 6
    Irish authors, 49
    Large-Print Books, 23
    My ABC's, 3
    New on the shelf, 24
    Open book, 2, 3, 4, 115
    Shamrocks, 49
    Small-books frame, 2
    Study guides, 40
    Three-ring binder, 7
Bunny, 117
Bunny in hat, 20

Bursts
    Large rectangular, 97
    Large round, 98
    Lightning bolts, 101
    Small rectangular, 99
    Small round, 100
Butterflies, 55, 118

Candy canes, 71
Captions
    A Winning Hand, 104
    Bookmobile, 41
    Books for children, 16
    Cassettes, 38
    Children's Programs, 17
    Classical recordings, 38
    Computer club, 9
    Concerts, recitals, 38
    Emerald Isle, 49
    Fall at the Library, 62
    Films & filmstrips, 10
    Four-leaf clover, 49
    Four of a Kind, 104
    Ghost Stories, 6
    Graduation Day, 57
    Happy Chanukah, 68
    Happy New Year, 45
    Here's a good trick! 20
    Holiday hours, 22
    Irish Authors, 49
    It's For You! 26
    Just Say "Know"! 18
    Large-Print Books, 23
    Let Freedom Ring! 60
    Library Programs, 15
    Magic Show, 20
    Mother's Day, 56
    Music Programs, 38
    My ABC's, 3, 114

Captions (*continued*)
   New Films! 11
   New on the shelf, 24
   New Records, 12
   Newspapers, 25
   Notes, 28
   President's Day, 46
   Recitals, 38
   Recordings, 38
   Spring at the Library, 50
   St. Patrick's Day, 49
   Story Hour, 16
   Study Guides, 40
   Summer Programs, 58
   Telephone Reference Service, 26
   That's the Ticket! 39
   Valentine's Day, 47
   Winter activities at the Library, 65
Cello, 38, 115
Chalkboard, 40
Chanukah, 68
Cherries, 46, 122
Children's
   Dinosaurs, 102, 124
   Graduation Day, 57
   Magic Show, 20
   My ABC's, 3
   Programs, 17
   Story hour, 16
   Teddy bears, 111
Christmas
   Candy canes, 71
   Gift boxes frame, 70
   Holly leaves, 69
   Santa Claus, 72, 122
Circus tents, 21
Classical music, 38
Clipboard, 29
Clock, 16, 115
Clouds, 52
Computers
   Computer club, 9
   Computer frame, 8

Daisies, 50, 118
Daisies frame, 53
Days of the week, 41
Desk pad, 33
Dinosaurs, 102, 124
Diploma, 57, 119

Exploding border, 103

Faces
   Bird in nest, 54
   Bunny, 117
   Bunny in hat, 20
   Children's heads, 17, 117
   Clock face, 16, 115
   Computer club, 9
   Flower face, 50, 118
   Ghost Stories, 6
   Santa Claus, 72, 122
   Smiling face, 109
   Smiling sun, 58, 120
   Snowman, 65
   Snowmen, 67
   Teddy bears, 111
   Woman silhouette, 56
Fall at the Library, 62
Fancy
   Ribbons frame, 95
   Victorian, 94
Film reels, 11, 114
Films & filmstrips, 10
Firecrackers, 59
Flowers, 53, 118
Four aces, 104
Four-leaf clovers, 49
Fruit, 122

Geometric designs, 75, 79, 81, 83, 123
Ghost Stories, 6
Gift boxes frame, 70
Girl, 56, 119
Globe, 35
Globe on stand, 105
Graduation Day, 57

Halloween, 63, 121
Hand, 91, 123
Hatchet, 46, 122
Hats, 46, 117, 119, 121, 122
Hearts
   Small-hearts frame, 48
   Valentine's Day, 47

Holidays
   Chanukah, 68
   Halloween, 63, 121
   Holiday hours, 22
   July 4th, 59
   New Year, 45
   President's Day, 46
   St. Patrick's Day, 49
   Thanksgiving, 64
   Valentine's Day, 47, 48
Holly, 69
Hourglasses, 45

Ice cream cones, 36, 116

Just Say "Know"! 18

Kites, 52
Klieg lights, 27

Large-Print Books, 23
Leaves, 62, 121
Liberty Bell, 60, 120
Library programs, 15
Library symbol, 14, 116
Lightning frame, 101
Lights, 27
List of services, 19

Magic Show, 20
Magnifying glass, 106
Mother's Day, 56
My ABC's, 3

New on the shelf, 24
New records, 12
New Year, 45
Newspapers, 25
Notes, 28
Nuts and bolts frame, 108

Old Fashioned
   "Sampler" frame, 74
Olive branch, 68
Open book, 4, 115

Paper clips, 33
Patriotic
   Liberty Bell, 60, 120
   Stars and Stripes, 61, 120
Patterns, 84, 88
Pencils, large, 107
Pencils, small, 110, 124
Periodicals
   Newspapers, 25
Piano, 37, 115
Picture frames, 32
Plain
   Oval frames, 93
   Round-cornered frames, 77
   Shaded rectangles, 76
   Shaded rectangular frames, 78
   Small oblong boxes, 92
   Small rectangles, 89
   Small squares, 90
President's Day, 46
Programs
   Children's Programs, 17
   Classical recordings, 38
   Concerts, recitals, 38
   Hand, painting frame, 91
   Klieg lights, 27
   Library programs, 15
   Magic Show, 20
   Music program, piano recital, 37
   Story hour, 16
   Theater tickets, 39
Pumpkins, 121

Rabbit. *See* Bunny.
Records, 12, 114
Reference
   Globe on stand, 105
   Globe with panels, 35
   Telephone reference, 26
Ribbons, 95, 117, 119

Sampler border, 74
Santa Claus, 72, 122
Seasonal
   Candy canes, 71
   Daisies, 50, 53, 118
   Fall at the Library, 62
   Gift boxes, 70
   Graduation Day, 57
   Halloween, 63, 121

Seasonal (*continued*)
  Happy Chanukah, 68
  Mother's Day, 56
  Pilgrim hats & pumpkins, 64, 121
  Santa Claus, 72, 122
  Spring at the Library, 50
  Summer at the Library, 58
  Winter activities at the Library, 65
Services, 19
Shamrocks, 49
Signpost, 34
Signs & Memos
  Blackboard, 40
  Bookmobile, 41
  Brochure layout, 42, 43
  Circus tents, 21
  Clipboard, 29
  Desk pad, 33
  Exploding frame, 103
  Four of a kind, 104
  Globe on stand, 105
  Globe with panels, 35
  Holiday hours, 22
  Ice cream cones, 36, 116
  Just Say "Know"! 18
  Library-symbol frame, 14
  Notes (ruled pad), 28
  Nuts and bolts frame, 108
  Pages in perspective, 30
  Pencils frame, 107
  Picture frames, 32
  Resources/services, 19
  Sign boards, 34
  Small-pencils frame, 110
  Smiling face, 109
  Spiral notebook, 31
  Theater tickets, 39
Silhouettes, 17, 117
Smiling face, 109
Snowflakes, 66, 122
Snowman, 65
Snowmen, 67
Spiral notebook, 31

Spring
  Bird-in-nest frame, 54
  Butterflies frame, 55
  Daisies, 50, 118
  Daisies frame, 53
  Kites, 52
  Mother's Day, 56
  Spring at the Library, 50
  St. Patrick's Day, 49
  Umbrellas, 51, 119
Star of David, 68
Stars, 61, 120
Story hour, 16
Summer
  Summer at the Library, 57
Sun, 58, 120

Teddy bears, 111
Telephone, 26, 114
Tents, 21
Thanksgiving, 64
Theater lights, 27
Theater tickets, 39
Three-ring binder, 7
Tickets, 39

Umbrellas, 51, 119
Umbrellas frame, 51

Valentine's Day, 47

Winter
  Happy Chanukah! 68
  Holly leaves, 69
  Santa Claus, 72, 122
  Snowflakes, 66, 122
  Snowmen frame, 67
  Winter activities at the Library, 65
Witches, 63, 121
World, 35